SCIENTIFIC BREAKTHROUGHS

Life Sciences

TEACHER RESOURCES

Edited by Tim Cooke

LIGHTBOX
openlightbox.com

LIGHTBOX

Go to
www.openlightbox.com
and enter this book's
unique code.

ACCESS CODE

LBXW8765

Lightbox is an all-inclusive digital solution for the teaching and learning of curriculum topics in an original, groundbreaking way. Lightbox is based on National Curriculum Standards.

STANDARD FEATURES OF LIGHTBOX

AUDIO High-quality narration using text-to-speech system

VIDEOS Embedded high-definition video clips

ACTIVITIES Printable PDFs that can be emailed and graded

WEBLINKS Curated links to external, child-safe resources

SLIDESHOWS Pictorial overviews of key concepts

TRANSPARENCIES Step-by-step layering of maps, diagrams, charts, and timelines

INTERACTIVE MAPS Interactive maps and aerial satellite imagery

QUIZZES Ten multiple choice questions that are automatically graded and emailed for teacher assessment

KEY WORDS Matching key concepts to their definitions

MORE Extra information and details on the subject

FIRST HAND Letters, diaries, and other primary sources

DOCS Speeches, newspaper articles, and other historical documents

Contents

RUBRIC

Conducting an Interview

Students will conduct an interview with a member of the scientific community about a significant discovery he or she made or important research he or she conducted. The student is to submit an audio recording and transcript of the interview. An exemplary interview will meet the following criteria.

- Clearly defines the purpose of the interview
- Conducts thorough background research to inform the focus of the interview and the questions
- Drafts a complete list of thoughtful, in-depth, and varied questions prior to the interview
- Interviews a subject with relevant knowledge on the topic and time period in question
- Asks questions in a logical order, building upon each other
- Treats the interview subject in a polite and professional manner
- Does not interrupt or rush the interview subject
- Shows interest and enthusiasm in responses and follow-up questions
- Chooses follow-up questions that demonstrate active listening
- Asks for clarification and further details when necessary
- Asks questions about personal experiences related to the topic
- Asks questions regarding factual information and the interview subject's opinion on the topic
- Asks creative questions that reflect fresh insights on the topic
- Records the full interview in a quiet environment
- Organizes and edits the interview transcript to be clear and factual

Introduction

The study of life fascinates humans. What makes something alive? What are the processes by which living things survive, reproduce, and then die? How can crops and animals be improved so they yield more grains, more meat, or more wool?

The Greek philosopher Aristotle thought there were about 500 different species of animal, and he tried to figure out why different animals had different body parts. His ideas were dominant in the Roman Empire and the Middle Ages. He argued that there was a "great chain of being" linking inanimate objects such as metals to plants, then animals, and then humans.

Around the world, societies had practical ideas about life sciences, mainly linked to agriculture and medicine. Then, during the early modern period in Europe, scientists began to figure out how the natural world fit together. Important work was done by men such as Carolus Linnaeus, who devised systems of classification. The great breakthrough came in the early 1800s when scientists realized that Earth was far older than they had ever imagined. Charles Darwin recognized that gradual change over huge time spans had resulted in all the life on Earth today. Then, in the twentieth century, the process in which these changes were caused by the combination and recombination of the DNA molecule was at last understood.

Carolus Linnaeus

Lapland, Finland

In 1732, Carolus Linnaeus spent six months in Lapland and discovered 100 new plants. To describe his discoveries, he devised a new system of classifying plants that is still in use today. He divided all plants into three kingdoms and further divided the family tree into individual **species**.

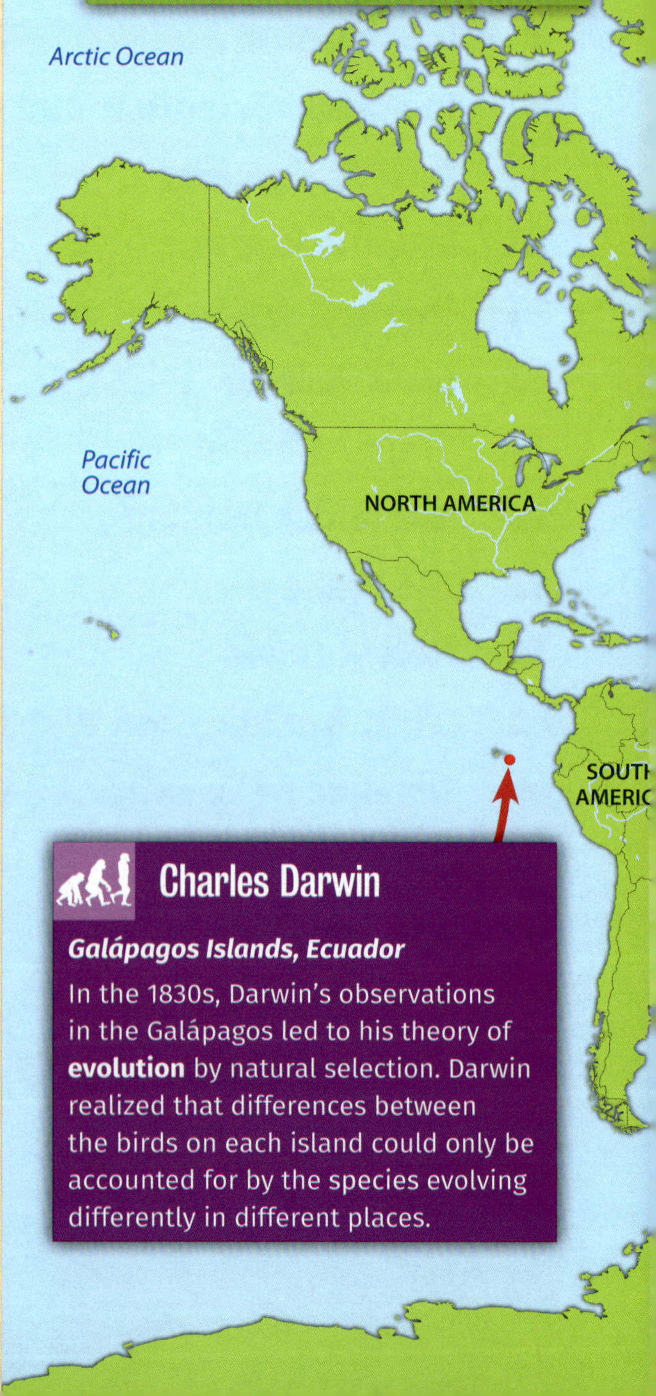

Charles Darwin

Galápagos Islands, Ecuador

In the 1830s, Darwin's observations in the Galápagos led to his theory of **evolution** by natural selection. Darwin realized that differences between the birds on each island could only be accounted for by the species evolving differently in different places.

Important Scientists and Discoveries

Franklin, Crick, and Watson

Cambridge, England

Scientists working at the Cavendish Laboratory in Cambridge in the 1950s made a crucial breakthrough. They realized that the DNA molecule was a double helix. The molecule combined and recombined as the building block through which living beings passed on characteristics to their offspring.

The Leakeys

Olduvai Gorge, Tanzania

The Leakey family's discoveries at this site in Tanzania transformed the understanding of human evolution. They realized that the first hominids had lived in Olduvai. The Leakeys plotted the major steps in human evolution from three million years ago, including physical adaptations, such as walking on two legs, and cultural advances, such as tool making.

EXTENSION ACTIVITY

Google Maps

Important Scientists and Discoveries

Explore these locations using street view to learn more about important scientists and their discoveries.

1. What do these locations have in common with each other? What are the differences between them?
2. Why are these discoveries associated with these specific locations? In your opinion, would the work of these scientists and their discoveries have been possible elsewhere? Support your opinions with examples.

Document

***The History of Animals*, Book I, Part I**

Examine the excerpt from *The History of Animals* by Aristotle.

1. What is the system of animal classification proposed by Aristotle? How does this system differ from the ones proposed in other historical periods? Why is Aristotle's classification different from later ones?
2. Why did Aristotle mention man among the other animals? What are the peculiar characteristics of man according to Aristotle?
3. Is Aristotle accurate in his descriptions of the "character" of the different animals? Why or why not?

CAROLUS LINNAEUS

1707–1778

Linnaeus laid the foundations for the modern system of classifying all living things. His method, called "binomial nomenclature," used just two names to identify every species. It is still employed today. Linnaeus is regarded as one of the greatest of all naturalists.

Carl Linnaeus was born in Råshult, Sweden, on May 23, 1707. Carl's father was a clergyman named Nils Ingemarsson, which means "Nils, the son of Ingemar," as was the custom in Scandinavia. When Nils became a student at Lund University, however, he had to add a formal surname in order to register. Latin names were fashionable, so he named himself Linnaeus after a type of lime tree that was called "linn" in the local dialect. When his son, Carl, began to publish his work, he took the Latinization further, calling himself Carolus Linnaeus.

Like many country parsons, Nils was an enthusiastic amateur botanist. Botany is the scientific study of plants. It was through his father that Carolus acquired his enthusiasm for the subject. By the time he was eight years old, the family had already nicknamed Linnaeus "the little botanist."

A Medical Education

When Carolus started high school, his parents hoped he would also become a clergyman. Linnaeus was a poor student, but he was good at Latin. Johan Rothman, a local doctor and teacher, noticed Linnaeus's interest in plants and gave him private lessons in medicine and botany. Rothman encouraged Linnaeus to give up studying religion, or theology, and take up medicine. In those days many medicines were derived from herbs, so botanical knowledge was useful for doctors. In 1727, Linnaeus enrolled as a medical student at the University of Lund. The following year, he moved to the University of Uppsala.

Classifying Plants

Uppsala University had a botanical garden, to which Linnaeus was soon drawn. It was there he met Olof Celsius, dean of Uppsala Cathedral and uncle of Anders Celsius, who devised the temperature scale that bears his name. Olof Celsius, who was also a botanist, was impressed with Linnaeus's knowledge of plants. He introduced him to Olof Rudbeck Jr., director of the botanical garden, who was looking for someone to take over from him.

Carolus Linnaeus's former home in Uppsala has been turned into a museum. It still houses many of the plant and animal specimens he collected.

In 1736, Linnaeus published *Hortus Cliffortianus*. Compiling the illustrated catalogue of a private garden gave Linnaeus ideas about classifying plants.

Rudbeck recognized Linnaeus's talent for botany. Even though Linnaeus was only in the second year of his studies, the director invited him to become a lecturer in botany. Linnaeus was especially interested in flower structure. Developing the ideas he had acquired from Rothman, he became convinced that it would be possible to introduce a new, much improved system for classifying plants based on their reproductive structures.

To Lapland

In 1732, Linnaeus set off on an expedition to Lapland, a wilderness inhabited by the Lapp people that spread over parts of Norway, Sweden, Finland, and Russia. He spent four months there, journeying thousands of miles on foot to the Arctic Ocean, and discovering about 100 new species of plants. His account of the expedition, *Flora Lapponica*, was published in 1737. In the report, Linnaeus first used the alchemical symbols for Venus and copper and for Mars and iron to denote "female" and "male," respectively.

EXTENSION ACTIVITY

Video

An introduction to: Taxonomy

Discover taxonomy and how biological classification works by watching this video.

1. What is biological classification? What is its purpose? Why is it important to categorize species? Defend your answer using examples.
2. What reasons could Linnaeus have had for using Latin in his binomial nomenclature? Why do we still use Latin for biological classification? Formulate some hypotheses.

Weblink

Studying Medicine: Training at the Faculty of Medicine in the 18th Century

Analyze the history of Uppsala University's Faculty of Medicine and assess its connection to Linnaeus.

1. What was the organization of the eighteenth-century faculty of medicine in Uppsala? How did this organization differ from a contemporary faculty of medicine? Provide examples to defend your ideas.
2. In your opinion, why did Linnaeus succeed in becoming a physician? Would he have followed a similar career path today? Why or why not? Formulate some hypotheses.

As a professor at Uppsala University, Linnaeus was in charge of a botanical garden that had been founded there nearly a century earlier.

Love Blossoms

Linnaeus was not only interested in **biology**. He studied all aspects of natural history, the name given at the time to the study of the natural world. In 1733, he gave lectures at Uppsala about the study of minerals, known as mineralogy. In 1734, Linnaeus traveled to the county of Dalarna to visit a copper mine. There he met a local doctor named Johan Moraeus and his daughter, Sara Elisabeth. Love blossomed between Linnaeus and Sara. The pair became engaged, though they did not actually marry until five years later.

Johan Moraeus had qualified as a doctor in the Netherlands, and he persuaded Linnaeus that he should do the same. In 1735, Linnaeus graduated as a doctor of medicine from the University of Harderwijk in the Netherlands. He then moved to the Dutch city of Leiden. There, he showed one of his manuscripts to a well-known botanist named Jan Frederik Gronovius. Gronovius was so impressed that he published Linnaeus's work at his own expense, under the title *Systema Naturae*. The book contained a list of plants, animals, and minerals classified according to a new scheme. Linnaeus's scheme aroused much interest among his fellow naturalists.

Linnaeus continued to travel around Europe. In 1737 he published *Genera Plantarum*, in which he expanded on his classification system for plants. The following year he visited Paris. He met many leading botanists, including the German Johann Dillenius, who was professor of botany at Oxford University in England, and the French botanist brothers Antoine and Bernard Jussieu.

Doctor And Scientist

Still just 31 years old, Linnaeus set himself up in practice as a physician. He was also admired for his scientific work. In 1739, he became a founding member and the first president of the Royal Swedish Academy of Sciences. He was also appointed physician to the Admiralty. In 1741, Linnaeus was first appointed professor of practical medicine at the University of Uppsala, but within a year he had become professor of botany.

Linnaeus's Legacy

Species Plantarum, published in 1753, is considered to be Linnaeus's most important work. It listed all the species known at the time according to his system of classification. The system was easy to use, enabling people to categorize species quickly.

Together with the fifth edition of *Genera Plantarum*, which appeared in 1754, *Species Plantarum* remains the starting point for the botanical naming of flowering plants and ferns. Linnaeus published about 180 books. He urged his students to visit every part of the world in search of new specimens. Twenty-three of his former students became professors. Their efforts helped Linnaeus spread his ideas to the leading European naturalists of the day. The king and queen of Sweden were among his patrons, and in 1761 he was made a nobleman. From then on he was known as Carl von Linné.

In 1774 Linnaeus suffered a stroke. He died at Uppsala on 22 January, 1778, and was buried in the cathedral in the city. His son, Carl Linnaeus the Younger, succeeded him in his post as professor of botany at Uppsala University. He continued to add to his father's unique botanical collection.

The collectors Linnaeus sent around the world discovered thousands of new species of plants.

PRESERVING THE PAST

The Linnean Society was founded in 1788. It is the world's oldest biological society. Its first president was Sir James Edward Smith, an English medical student and naturalist. In 1783, Smith bought Linnaeus's collection of manuscripts and specimens from the botanist's widow in Sweden. She needed the money to provide money for her four daughters to get married. Smith initially rented rooms in London, where he displayed the collection to a curious public.

The first meeting of the Linnean Society was held at Smith's home on April 8, 1788. Its aim was "the cultivation of the science of Natural History." The society remains a key place for discussion on many aspects of science. In 1829, after Smith's death, the society bought the Linnean and Smith collections and libraries. More than 40,000 specimens from Linnaeus's collection are preserved in its London headquarters, alongside several other major plant and animal collections. The society also houses an important library. The library specializes in works on the classification system that Linnaeus had successfully standardized.

EXTENSION ACTIVITY

More

Botanical Gardens

Review the origins of botanical gardens and their evolution.

1. Besides the rebirth of interest in science, what other events could have influenced the development of botanical gardens during the sixteenth century? Research the other possible reasons and support your answer with examples.
2. What was the purpose of botanical gardens at the time? Do botanical gardens have the same purpose today? Formulate and explain your hypothesis with examples.

Weblink

The Linnaean Herbarium

Explore the herbarium of Linnaeus using the online research tool.

1. What was the original purpose of Linnaeus's herbarium? How might contemporary scientists use Linnaeus's herbarium in a different way than he used it? Formulate some hypotheses.
2. Why might Linnaeus's herbarium have been digitized? Is Linnaeus's research still current and useful for contemporary scientists? Why or why not?

EDWARD JENNER

1749–1823

In 1980, smallpox, a disease that had killed thousands of people each year, was eliminated thanks to a global **vaccination** campaign. This was possible thanks to an experiment carried out 200 years earlier by Edward Jenner, an English country doctor.

Edward Jenner helped save the lives of millions of humans by preventing a terrible disease. Indirectly, he also laid the foundations for virology, the study of **viruses**. Jenner was born on May 17, 1749, in Berkeley, Gloucestershire, England. In 1770, he traveled to London to study surgery and anatomy, which is the physical structure of animals and plants, under the Scottish surgeon John Hunter. In London, Jenner was also employed by the famous naturalist Sir Joseph Banks. Banks had sailed with the British explorer, Captain James Cook, as the official naturalist on Cook's first expedition to the Southern Hemisphere from 1768 to 1771. Jenner helped Banks sort the specimens he had collected in Australia, New Zealand, and islands in the Pacific.

In 1773, Jenner returned to Berkeley, where he stayed for the rest of his life. He set up practice as a physician, and in 1788, married Catharine Kingscote. In 1792, he was awarded a medical degree by the University of St. Andrews in Scotland.

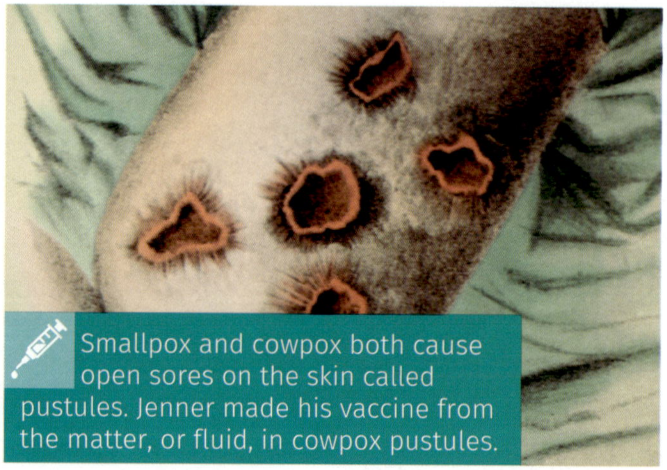

Smallpox and cowpox both cause open sores on the skin called pustules. Jenner made his vaccine from the matter, or fluid, in cowpox pustules.

Jenner began his investigations of the link between cowpox and smallpox when he heard a folk tale that milkmaids never got smallpox.

No one knows when smallpox first infected humans, but it was known in Africa and Asia by around 1000 BC. The disease probably reached Europe in the 500s. In 570 AD, Bishop Marius of Avenches called the illness "variola," which is Latin for "pox," and this became its scientific name. The disease was fatal, and those who survived it could often be disfigured and blinded by its effects. Many were pockmarked, their bodies and especially their faces covered with scars and pits marking the places where there had been blisters. In extreme cases, pockmarks could almost destroy faces.

A Risky Treatment

In the eighteenth century, smallpox was a common and much feared disease. Many people died during smallpox epidemics. At the time, the only method of fighting the disease was **inoculation**. Inoculation involves implanting a mild form of a disease in a healthy person. This allows the person's body to build up a natural resistance to the disease. In the case of smallpox, "matter" from the blisters on a person with a mild attack was injected into the patient. Inoculation was risky, however. An inoculated patient could get a serious case of the disease. They could also pass on the infection to other people.

Cowpox and Folklore

By 1775, Jenner had become interested in smallpox and its link with cowpox. Cowpox was a similar disease, but much less severe. It affects cows, and milkmaids often caught it from infected cows. People who survived smallpox never caught it again. Even the mildest smallpox infection made a person resistant to the disease, or "immune." There was a folk belief near Jenner's home that cowpox sometimes had the same effect, giving milkmaids who had suffered it **immunity** against smallpox. Jenner found that there are two forms of cowpox, but only one protects against smallpox. He also found that cowpox only protects against smallpox if a person gets it at the right stage in its development.

EXTENSION ACTIVITY

More

Symptoms of Smallpox and the origins of Inoculation

Examine the main symptoms of smallpox, and the origins of inoculation.

1. Why was it difficult to prevent smallpox infection prior to the invention of the smallpox inoculation process? Why were Mexican Indian and Native North Americans particularly affected by smallpox? Besides inoculation, what else could have prevented the spreading of the disease brought by European colonists? Formulate some theories.
2. Why do you think inoculation was seldom used before Edward Jenner's work on the smallpox vaccination? Propose some hypotheses.

First Hand

A Letter of Edward Jenner (1749–1823)

Review the letter written by Edward Jenner to Edward Loveden on April 17, 1805.

1. Why did Edward Jenner write the letter? How does the content of the letter relate to Edward Jenner's research on smallpox?
2. In what terms did Edward Jenner describe smallpox? What could the role of government be in preventing the diffusion of smallpox contagion, according to Edward Jenner? Would this proposal have been effective? Why or why not?

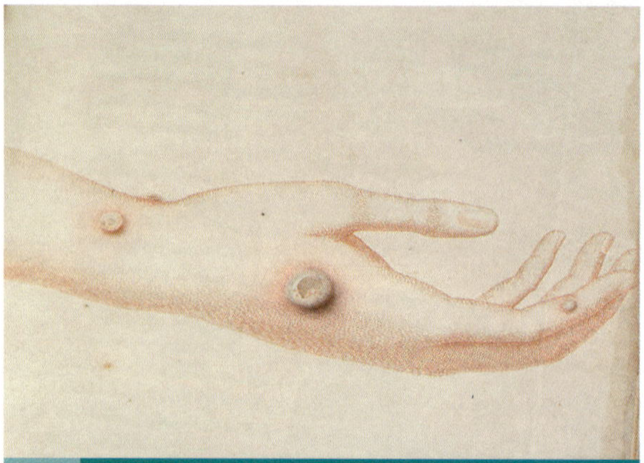

The milkmaid Sarah Nelmes developed cowpox from being in contact with cows' udders. Jenner used material from her sores to inject his first patient.

Jenner also found that being exposed to a disease of horses called "the grease" gave people immunity to smallpox. In 1788, Gloucestershire was struck by a smallpox epidemic. As Jenner traveled about, treating patients, he was struck by the fact that people who had suffered from cowpox in the past did not show symptoms of smallpox, despite being exposed to it. He suspected that inoculation with cowpox would be an effective and safer form of preventive medicine than inoculation with live smallpox.

A Milkmaid Lends a Hand

There were few cowpox cases in the region at that time, but in 1796, Jenner found a milkmaid with the telltale blisters on her hands. On May 14, 1796, he performed the first inoculation with cowpox on a young patient called James Phipps. Jenner made small cuts in James's arm and worked into them a small amount of material from the milkmaid's blisters. James suffered a mild fever, but soon recovered. In July, Jenner inoculated James again, but this time with matter from a smallpox victim. James remained healthy.

Jenner repeated the experiment in 1798. The second trial was also successful, and Jenner reported his findings to the Royal Society. Some members of the society advised Jenner not to risk his reputation by challenging established opinion. So Jenner published his paper privately under the title, "Inquiry into the Causes and Effects of the Variolae Vaccinae." "Vacca" is the Latin name for cow. Jenner used it to come up with the word "vaccination" to describe inoculation with cowpox matter. Inoculation with smallpox, or variola, matter is known as "variolation." Although Jenner had found a way to protect people against smallpox, he had no idea why it worked. That discovery came much later.

Vaccination Saves Many Lives

Within a few years, vaccination was being practiced widely. In 1802, Parliament gave Jenner a large grant to help his work. Jenner vaccinated the poor free of charge. A Royal Jennerian Society was established in 1803 to promote vaccination in London. The average annual death rate from smallpox in London fell from 2,018 to 622. The Royal College of Physicians reported favorably on vaccination in 1807, and the British government was moved to increase Jenner's grant.

Jenner became famous worldwide. In parts of Germany, his birthday was made a holiday. The French emperor Napoleon Bonaparte was impressed by Jenner's work. When some British civilians were captured by the French, Jenner was among those who signed a petition for their release. Napoleon freed the prisoners. Britain was relatively slow to recognize Jenner's achievement, although the University of Oxford awarded him an honorary doctorate of medicine in 1813. Jenner published his last work on vaccination in 1822. Jenner died from a stroke on January 26, 1823.

James Phipps was eight years old when Jenner vaccinated him with cowpox. Phipps had never had smallpox, so was not immune to the disease.

SMALLPOX ERADICATION

Scientists now know that smallpox, or Variola, is spread by a virus. The Variola virus has one weakness. It can live and multiply only in humans. That means that if the virus could be eliminated from the human population, smallpox would be "eradicated," or destroyed for ever. By the middle of the twentieth century, vaccination programs had made smallpox a rare disease in Europe, North America, Australia, and New Zealand. In countries that could not afford to vaccinate everyone, however, the disease was still common. In 1967, the World Health Organization, or WHO, an agency of the United Nations, launched a World Eradication Program against smallpox. It made vaccination programs available all over the world, and asked all governments to report any smallpox cases in their countries. Success came swiftly. In 1966, the year before the program started, between 10 and 15 million people died from smallpox worldwide. Within a decade, the number of cases had fallen dramatically. The last recorded case was in Somalia, in Africa, in 1977. In 1979, the WHO declared smallpox to have been eradicated throughout Africa. In 1980, it was able to announce that the disease had been eliminated throughout the world.

EXTENSION ACTIVITY

More

Jan Ingenhousz (1730–1799)
Examine the life and scientific activity of Jan Ingenhousz.

1. Why did Jan Ingenhousz oppose Jenner's championing of vaccination? What arguments can be made for or against vaccination today? Explain and defend a position using evidence found in the library or on the internet.
2. In your opinion, why was Ingenhousz an expert in both medicine and botany? Would scientists be able to master different subjects of expertise today? Why or why not?

Weblink

Save Smallpox! The Conservation of One of the World's Deadliest Diseases
Evaluate the ideas expressed by the blog post about the conservation of smallpox virus.

1. What is the position of the author about the conservation of the smallpox virus? Do you agree or disagree with the author? Defend your opinion.
2. If smallpox has been eradicated, why would scientists choose to continue researching this virus? Formulate some hypotheses.
3. Is the use of smallpox as a bioweapon an actual threat? Why or why not? Support your point of view with examples.

CHARLES DARWIN

1809–1882

Charles Darwin, together with Alfred Russel Wallace, showed how the characteristics of species developed over long periods. The proposal, known as the theory of evolution by natural selection, revolutionized how people viewed the world and themselves.

Charles Darwin was born in Shrewsbury, England, on February 12, 1809. He showed an interest in science, and in 1825, he went to study medicine at the University of Edinburgh. Darwin also studied theology at Cambridge University, but his real interest was natural history. While at Cambridge he met many eminent scientists. One, Adam Sedgwick, was a professor of geology, the study of Earth's rocks. In 1831, Darwin accompanied Sedgwick on a field excursion to Wales, which was the only time Darwin ever received formal scientific training. Darwin graduated from medicine in 1831. Meanwhile, in London, Captain Robert Fitzroy was preparing an expedition on his ship HMS *Beagle* to survey the coasts of South America for the Royal Navy. Fitzroy advertised for a "well-educated and scientific person" to join the voyage. Darwin applied for the post and was chosen.

Charles Darwin lived for over 40 years at Down House in Kent. It was here that he developed his theories about evolution and how it occurred.

The Birth of a New Science

Until the 1700s, people believed that Earth was only a few thousand years old. However, some scientists speculated that Earth's history was much longer. In 1795, Scottish scientist James Hutton suggested that Earth had changed very slowly over millions of years, and was still changing. By the early 1800s, Scottish geologist Charles Lyell had reached the same conclusion as Hutton. Hutton and Lyell's theories met with strong resistance, but Darwin was impressed by them. What he saw over the years of the *Beagle*'s voyage persuaded him that Lyell's theories were correct.

Changing Plants and Animals

Christians believed that God had made animals and plants in a "Great Chain of Being," at the top of which was humankind. By the end of the 1700s, some people were increasingly questioning these views. They included Charles's grandfather, Erasmus Darwin, and the French naturalist Chevalier de Lamarck, known as Jean Baptiste Pierre Antoine de Monet. Lamarck proposed a way in which species might change.

The naval ship HMS *Beagle* was one of the first vessels to have a lightning conductor to prevent it from being damaged in electrical storms.

He suggested that over generations, species become better adapted to their environments. Lamarck believed the frequent use of an organ would enlarge and strengthen it. For example, he thought a giraffe's neck would lengthen as it stretched for leaves on high trees. Lamarck believed that this "long-neckedness" would be passed on to the next generation. Although the theory Darwin developed on the voyage of the *Beagle* was similar to Lamarck's, it has significant differences.

The Voyage of the *Beagle*

In December 1831, the *Beagle* left port. When the ship anchored at Saint Jago in the Cape Verde Islands, off the coast of West Africa, the rock strata there provided Darwin with evidence to support the idea of slow change described in Lyell's book.

EXTENSION ACTIVITY

More

Layers of History

Analyze the principle of superposition and its importance for geology.

1. With the invention of modern dating techniques, is the principle of superposition still relevant? Why or why not? Support your answer with research found in the library or on the internet.
2. Why is it important to date geological strata? Are there other scientific disciplines relying on the principle of superposition or on similar principles for dating?

Weblink

Early concepts of Evolution: Jean Baptiste de Lamarck

Explore Jean Baptiste de Lamarck's theory of evolution.

1. What are the principles of evolution defined by Lamarck? In what ways did these principles differ from the theories of other eighteenth-century scientists? Why might this have occurred?
2. How are Lamarck's and Darwin's theories different? Could either of their theories be considered outdated today? Why? Support your answer with examples.

RUBRIC

Create a Scientific Drawing

Create a scientific drawing illustrating an object or design. An exemplary scientific drawing will meet the following criteria.

- Includes a descriptive and accurate title
- The drawing(s) realistically depicts the object(s)
- The drawing only includes features that were actually observed
- Relevant details such as size, colors, textures, shapes, and relationships to surroundings are included
- Multiple perspectives are drawn to provide the viewer with a complete picture
- All parts of the scientific drawing are clearly labeled with the correct terms
- A written explanation of the drawing shows what is included in the drawing
- A key or legend is provided
- An appropriate size and scale is chosen for the drawing so that the details are easily recognized

HMS *Beagle* surveyed the South American coast from 1831 to 1836. The red line indicates the ship's route. It was one of the most important scientific voyages of all time. The ship also visited the Galápagos Islands. There, Darwin studied local birds and found evidence to support his theories about natural selection.

Darwin found a layer of limestone nearly 45 feet (14 meters) above sea level that contained seashells. Clearly, either the sea was once much higher or the land was once lower. From here the *Beagle* crossed to Brazil and down the Brazilian coast to Rio de Janeiro.

Darwin was transfixed by everything he saw. He collected and sent home hundreds of specimens. "You cannot imagine what a fine miser-like pleasure I enjoy," he wrote, "when examining an animal differing widely from any known genus [type]."

Next, the *Beagle* set sail for Patagonia. There, Darwin found a 20-foot (6-m) high cliff embedded with huge bones, which he realized belonged to animals far bigger than any now in existence. These were the remains of giant sloths, giant armadillos, and other creatures. He saw that they resembled similar modern, much smaller species, and wondered why the giant species had died out.

The Moving Earth

In July 1834, Darwin explored the Chilean Andes. He found **fossil** seashells at an altitude of 12,000 feet (3,658 m). This confirmed what Darwin was thinking. The region must once have been beneath the sea but had later been pushed up above sea level. The mountains would first have appeared as islands in the sea, and eventually raised to form mountains. On February 20, 1835, an earthquake in Chile destroyed the city of Concepción. Darwin noticed that the level of the land had risen after the earthquake. A new island had emerged in the ocean. To Darwin this was proof that land could rise up from the sea and form mountain ranges.

In October 1836, the *Beagle* arrived back in England. Some of Darwin's reports had been published while he was away, and he returned to find himself a leading scientific figure. On his return to England, Darwin began sorting the many specimens he had brought back. He also started to prepare his record of the voyage, which was published in 1839.

Evolution by Natural Selection

In 1837 Darwin became the secretary of the Geological Society, and in 1839 he was elected a fellow of the Royal Society. In June 1842 he wrote a draft of what would become his theory of evolution by natural selection.

The 19 islands of the Galápagos are separated from their neighbors by the ocean. Darwin concluded that animals on each island had also evolved separately.

EXTENSION ACTIVITY

First Hand

Charles Darwin's *Beagle* Diary
Analyze Charles Darwin's journal entries for October 1832.

1. What were the life conditions on the *Beagle*? How did Charles Darwin describe the travel and the stop-overs? How might these conditions have differed had Darwin completed the same journey today?
2. In what terms are the animals described in the journal entries? What did Charles Darwin note about the fossils he encountered? Why? Develop some hypotheses.

Weblink

Darwin's Finches and Natural Selection in the Galápagos
Examine the connection between Darwin's theory and the conservation of an endangered species.

1. How are Galápagos finches and Darwin's theory of evolution connected? How does Darwin's study of Galápagos finches help the modern conservation of this species?
2. If Galápagos finches are known to be the world's fastest-evolving vertebrates, why would they not adapt to avoid the parasitic flies which are now menacing their existence? Defend your ideas with evidence and reasoning.

The beaks of the finches on the different Galápagos Islands are different shapes, depending on their most important source of food.

Two years later, Darwin wrote a second draft. He then revised the journal, as well as writing other journals. In 1856, he started to write a complete statement of his ideas.

The Same Conclusion

Darwin had written about half of the book by the middle of 1858. On June 18 he received a copy of an essay written by the Welsh naturalist, Alfred Russel Wallace. Darwin realized that Wallace had reached the same conclusion as he had about the way species evolve, or change.

Both men saw that, within each species, some individuals have a characteristic that makes their survival more likely. The individuals pass this feature on to their offspring. Because the individuals are more likely to survive and breed, each generation gradually becomes more adapted to its environment.

Although Darwin had formed his theory years earlier, he decided to announce his theory at the same time as Wallace's. They agreed that a joint paper would be presented to the Linnean Society in London on July 1, 1858. Darwin also published a shorter account of his theory in a book called *On the Origin of Species by Means of Natural Selection, or The Preservation of Favoured Races in the Struggle for Life*. The first edition of 1,250 copies, published on November 26, 1859, sold out on the first day.

Darwin admitted that his theory presented difficulties. In particular, he had no idea how a characteristic, or variation, could emerge within a species or how characters could be from one generation to the next. He suggested the environment might stimulate variation in a way similar to that proposed by Lamarck. It was not until the work of Gregor Mendel later in the century that the principles of **genetics** began to be understood.

The Theory of Evolution

When scientists speak of "the theory of evolution," they mean the one put forward by Darwin and Wallace, in which natural selection is the mechanism that drives the evolution of species. Evolution is a process of gradual change. The word "evolution" describes the descent of **organisms** from one generation to another with slight modification until they are so different from their ancestors that they make up a new species.

The Darwinian, or Darwin-Wallace, theory has seven steps. First, individuals resemble their parents. Second, all individuals belonging to a species are slightly different from one another. Third, members of each generation usually produce more offspring than are needed to replace their parents.

Fourth, despite this, populations tend to remain stable and do not increase in size indefinitely. Fifth, since populations remain stable, not all offspring can survive. That means the offspring must compete to survive. Next, the survivors will be those individuals that differ in ways that allow them to use the resources available to them more efficiently. Finally, environmental conditions change over long periods of time. These changes naturally select the variations within a species that are best suited to them. Such changes also encourage new variations to emerge. Eventually, the variations are so marked that a completely new species is formed. Natural selection, through changing environmental conditions, causes new species to emerge.

Religious Objections

Darwin avoided the question of human evolution in *On the Origin of Species*, but his theory of natural selection disturbed people.

Darwin deliberately wrote *On the Origin of Species* to be accessible to general readers.

Religious opponents criticized it for suggesting that human intelligence developed naturally from characteristics already present in animals. They said that went against the belief that God placed humans above the animals.

Charles Darwin died in 1882 of heart failure. After a public petition, he was buried in Westminster Abbey. His grave is close to the tomb of Sir Isaac Newton.

ALFRED RUSSEL WALLACE (1828–1913)

In 1854, the naturalist Alfred Russel Wallace explored the East Indies, or Indonesia. He noticed differences in the region's animals. Those in the western islands resembled species found on the Asian mainland, and those in the eastern islands resembled Australian species. The groups are separated by a line between the islands of Borneo and Celebes, now called Sulawesi, and Bali and Lombok. The line is now called Wallace's Line. It follows a deepwater channel. Animals on either side of the channel have been isolated from each other for a long time.

In 1855, Wallace wrote a paper called "On the Law Which Has Regulated the Introduction of New Species." In it, he said that he often thought about how species change. In 1858, Wallace found himself thinking about Thomas Malthus's *An Essay on the Principle of Population*. In Wallace's own words, "There suddenly flashed upon me the idea of the survival of the fittest." Wallace wrote down his idea and mailed it to Darwin. Darwin recognized that he and Wallace had both reached the same conclusion, that evolution occurred by natural selection.

EXTENSION ACTIVITY

Weblink

Overview: The Conflict Between Religion and Evolution
Review the article about the conflict between religion and evolution.

1. What is the general tone of the article? How does the article present the debate and the two opposing points of view?
2. In your opinion, why is Darwin's theory still sparking debate more than 150 years after *On the Origin of Species* was published? Formulate some hypotheses.
3. Why did some U.S. states promulgate laws for prohibiting the teaching of evolution? Why did the U.S. Supreme Court limit these kinds of laws? Debate the possible reasons for both positions.

Video

The Wallace Line
Examine a video discussing the Wallace Line and the research associated to it.

1. What is the Wallace Line? How did the difference between the species on the two sides of the Line develop? Define the Line and explain the process of its development in your own words.
2. What scientific disciplines have been employed for the study of the Wallace Line? Why?

LOUIS PASTEUR

1822–1895

French chemist Louis Pasteur demonstrated that infectious diseases are caused by tiny organisms called **germs**. He found ways of preventing disease through "**pasteurization**" and developed vaccines for lethal diseases like rabies and anthrax.

Born on December 27, 1822, in Dole, France, Louis Pasteur entered the Collège Communal at Arbois in 1829. He was not a brilliant pupil, and his early ambition was to become an art teacher. In 1840, he graduated in arts from the Royal College in the city of Besançon, and in 1842 he graduated in science. He entered the École Normale Supérieure in 1843, to train as a teacher. As part of his studies, he attended lectures at the Sorbonne, which is part of the University of Paris. Pasteur was inspired by lectures given by the organic chemist Jean Baptiste André Dumas. As Pasteur's enthusiasm for chemistry grew, so his grades improved. He graduated as a doctor of science in 1847.

An Early Honor

Pasteur's early scientific interests lay in the field of crystallography, the study of the structure of crystals. He carried out detailed research into tartaric acid crystals. He discovered such crystals have particular qualities when they transmit polarized light, which is light in which the wave vibrations are arranged in a single plane. Pasteur's discovery laid the foundations for an important new branch of science called stereochemistry. Stereochemistry is the study of the way atoms are arranged within molecules.

Pasteur presented his results to the Paris Academy of Sciences. In recognition of his achievements he was awarded the ribbon of the Légion d'Honneur in 1853. In the meantime, he had met and married the daughter of the rector of the University of Strasbourg, Marie Laurent.

Developing Pasteurization

In 1854, Pasteur became the dean and a professor of chemistry at the University of Lille in France. He became interested in **fermentation**, a process that changes sugars in certain foods into alcohol. Brewers used a fungus called yeast to brew beer. At the time people believed that dead yeast **cells** helped fermentation in a chemical process. Instead, Pasteur found that fermentation is a biological process. "Live" yeast causes fermentation by feeding on sugars and producing alcohol as well as carbon dioxide gas.

In 1856, a local industrialist asked Pasteur to investigate why wine and beer turn sour. Examining beer under a microscope, Pasteur found that good beer contained round yeast cells and the sour beer had rod-like cells. There were two types of yeast. In the sour beer, the yeast that produced alcohol was contaminated by other yeast cells to produce acetic acid, or vinegar. Pasteur found that souring could be prevented by heating beer or wine to 122° Fahrenheit (50° Celsius), then sealing the container. The heating kills all the yeast, including the type that makes acetic acid. Pasteur deduced that the yeast that made acetic acid entered the beer from the air. He showed that **microorganisms** carried in the air were responsible for causing foods to ferment or to rot and decay. Pasteurization, the process of controlled heating named for Pasteur, kills these microorganisms. It is widely used today to preserve foods. Milk is pasteurized, for example, to destroy the **bacteria** that form lactic acid.

When grape juice ferments, the sugar in the juice turns to alcohol, producing wine. If the process is allowed to continue too long, however, the wine becomes sour.

161.6° F (72°C)
The temperature to which milk needs to be heated for 15 seconds to complete the **Pasteurization process.**

Growing **anthrax bacilli** at **107°F (42°C)** made them unable to produce **spores.**

In **1886** Pasteur treated **350** people who had been bitten by rabid dogs with his anti-rabies vaccine. **Only 1 developed rabies.**

EXTENSION ACTIVITY

Weblink

Got milk? How Pasteur made mass food production possible
Analyze the article describing the implications of pasteurization for the modern food industry.

1. Why might Pasteur have become a symbol of patriotism for France? Formulate some theories.
2. How are Pasteur's work and Darwin's theory correlated? What was the outcome of this correlation? Support your answer with evidence.

Document

Action de l'oxygène de l'air sur le vin.
Examine the 1866 plate by P. Lackerbauer and annotated by Louis Pasteur.

1. What does the drawing represent? To whom were Pasteur's annotations addressed?
2. What was the purpose of this plate? In 1866, which other ways of representing Pasteur's research were available?
3. How have the means of documenting a scientific research evolved over time? Support your answer with examples.

RUBRIC

Analyzing a Magazine Article

Students will assess a magazine article and write an analysis. An exemplary analysis will meet the following criteria.

- Identifies the topic of the article
- Identifies the main points and opinions presented in the article
- Identifies the writer of the article
- Presents information about the writer and infers how his or her life may have shaped this opinion
- Assesses the writer's reliability
- Analyzes how the writer makes his or her argument
- Uses evidence from the article to show how the writer supports his or her argument
- Analyzes the writer's use of literary devices to enhance the article
- Differentiates between the facts and opinions presented in the article
- Identifies when and where the article was published, and determines its intended audience
- Identifies and understands the goals of the article
- Assesses the effectiveness of the format in presenting the writer's argument
- Connects the article to the societal and historical context in which it was written
- Infers what is not said about this topic in the article
- Identifies what information is unintentionally implied in the article

Rabies is most often spread to humans by the bites of infected dogs. The disease has been largely eradicated in the Western world.

Saving the Silkworms

In the 1860s, the French silk industry was devastated by a disease that killed silkworms. Silkworms are actually the larvae of a species of moth. In 1865, Pasteur was asked to investigate the problem. He discovered the insects were suffering from two diseases caused by tiny parasites. Parasites live in or on other animals or plants, known as hosts, and get their nourishment from them. Pasteur found these parasites in the debris of the mulberry leaves on which the silkworms fed, and in the bodies of infected silkworms.

Combining this discovery with his earlier work, Pasteur developed the germ theory of disease. At the time, people believed disease was spread by poisonous fumes, or miasma, from dung heaps and decaying material.

Pasteur's new theory was that disease was caused by microorganisms. It gave people hope that these organisms could somehow be prevented from invading the body. That would stop so many people getting sick.

Preventing Chicken Cholera

In 1878, Pasteur began working on cases of chicken cholera, a fatal disease in chickens. He isolated the germ, a microorganism called a bacterium. He left some bacteria while he went on vacation. Then he injected the bacterium cultures into chickens. Pasteur found that the chickens did not get the disease and that they were resistant to infection by a fresh culture. Eventually Pasteur discovered that leaving the culture exposed to air at about 99°F (37°C) led to a weak form of the disease developing. Injected into chickens, the weakened disease made them immune to chicken cholera. Pasteur also made a vaccine to protect livestock against anthrax.

Finding a Cure for Rabies

Pasteur began one of his most famous pieces of research in 1882. He aimed to find a way of combating rabies, a disease that can be passed from infected dogs or other animals to humans through a bite. Once symptoms appear, the disease is usually fatal. After failed experiments with inoculations made from the saliva of animals infected with rabies, Pasteur concluded that the germ responsible was present in the brain and spinal column. It later became known that rabies is a virus, but they had not yet been discovered. Eventually, Pasteur developed a weakened form of the infection that he could use for inoculation. Pasteur had successfully treated animals with his vaccine, when he was unexpectedly presented with a human subject. On July 6, 1885, a nine-year-old boy named Joseph Meister was badly bitten by a dog with rabies.

The boy's mother begged Pasteur to inoculate him. Since the boy would almost certainly have died within a month, Pasteur agreed to try out his vaccine. Joseph survived, and since then the Pasteur vaccine has been used to prevent the onset of rabies in many thousands of people who have been infected.

A Fitting Tribute

The success of his rabies vaccine brought Pasteur great fame. He had been made a member of the French Academy of Medicine in 1873, and in 1874 the French National Assembly awarded him a pension for life. Many people regarded Pasteur as a national hero, and the French public raised money to help Pasteur in his work. In 1888, the Pasteur Institute opened in Paris. This was a private research laboratory dedicated to investigating rabies and preventing its spread. Pasteur was its first director. More branches of the institute opened in other parts of France and elsewhere. Louis Pasteur died at Saint-Cloud, near Paris, on September 28, 1895.

Louis Pasteur was buried in an elaborately tiled tomb at the Pasteur Institute in Paris, where he was a director until he died.

THE BATTLE AGAINST INFECTION

The causes of infection were not understood in the early 1800s, so protecting against germs was nearly impossible. The English nurse Florence Nightingale thought that the disease was caused by unpleasant fumes. She encouraged cleanliness, fresh air, and minimal furnishings in her wards. This helped to reduce germs.

Semmelweis, Lister, and Antisepsis

The Hungarian obstetrician Ignaz Semmelweis was dismayed at how many women died of fever around childbirth. He figured out that students who came from the dissecting room to treat patients must be carrying infection. When he told the students to wash their hands in disinfectant, the death rate among the patients dropped dramatically. This process of destroying germs is called antisepsis. **Antiseptics** were developed further in the late 1800s by the English surgeon Joseph Lister (below).

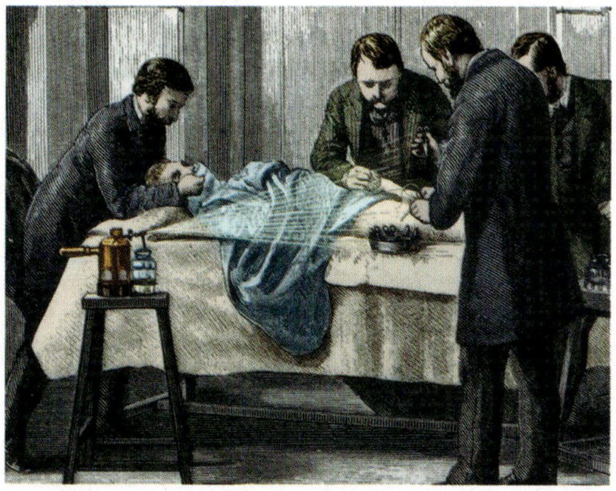

EXTENSION ACTIVITY

Weblink

Timeline of Vaccines

Analyze the timeline of vaccines from The College of Physicians of Philadelphia.

1. The introduction to the timeline states that the history of vaccine did not begin with the first vaccine. Do you agree with this statement? Why or why not? Defend your opinion.
2. Why does the timeline start with a sixteenth-century event? Formulate some theories.
3. What are the most important breakthroughs in the development of vaccines? When did they happen? Why might they have happened at these specific moments?

Document

Miss Nightingale Dies, Aged Ninety.

Examine the 1910 obituary for Florence Nightingale published in *The New York Times*.

1. What contribution did Florence Nightingale make in the battle against infection mentioned in the obituary? How are the professional accomplishments and achievements of Florence Nightingale described in the obituary? In your opinion, why are they described in these terms?
2. How might Florence Nightingale's contributions to the scientific advancements against germs have looked had she been allowed to study medicine? Formulate some hypotheses.

RUBRIC

Answer a Scientific Question

Students will define a scientific question or problem, and carry out an investigation or experiment to answer it, then write a report on their findings. An exemplary report will meet the following criteria.

- Problem is written in the form of a question with a question mark at the end
- Hypothesis is written as a guess or explanation to the answer of the problem
- Hypothesis is written in a complete sentence (for example, "I think ...," "I hypothesize ...," "If..., then...")
- Variable and controls are clearly identified
- Procedure steps are in numbered order
- Procedure steps show what to measure and where to record the data
- Procedure steps are written in complete sentences
- Data is organized in a data table
- The investigation or experiment includes more then one trial
- All numbers have labels
- All calculations are complete
- Conclusion is written in complete sentences
- Conclusion states whether the hypothesis was right or wrong
- Conclusion answers the question written in the problem

Gregor Mendel, an Austrian monk, investigated how inherited characteristics are passed from one generation of plants to another. His work led eventually to the discovery of **genes**, the units of inheritance. This made possible the study of genetics.

GREGOR MENDEL

1822–1884

Johann Mendel was born on July 22, 1822, in Hynčice in what is now the Czech Republic. He later changed his first name to Gregor. Mendel's parents were farmers, and his interest in agriculture, botany, and horticulture was first stimulated by his life on the family farm. It soon became obvious that Mendel was very intelligent. In 1841, he enrolled at the Philosophical Institute in Olmütz, now Olomouc, hoping to become a teacher. A farming accident in 1838 had left Mendel's father unable to work. As the only son, Mendel was expected to return home and take on the farm. Instead, he joined the priesthood, which would allow him to continue studying science. In 1843, Mendel entered the Augustinian monastery in Brno, taking the name of Gregor.

Gregor Mendel spent most of his career living and working at the monastery in Brno. At the time, the town was known as Brünn.

Encouraged to Learn

During the nineteenth century there was a big growth of interest in the natural sciences, such as biology and geology. It became common for leading citizens to set up local societies to promote scientific research. Among them was the abbot, or head, of Mendel's monastery, which had a well-stocked library and provided ideal conditions for studying. Abbot Napp allowed Mendel to continue to study science while he was preparing for the priesthood. Mendel was ordained in 1847. Soon after, he failed his exams to become a teacher. Napp sent the young priest to the University of Vienna where, from 1851 until 1853, Mendel studied a wide range of scientific subjects. In 1854, he returned to the monastery.

Unreliable Experiments

At the time, Brno was a center of the textile industry. However, the textile producers had to import high-quality wool from Spain. People tried to improve local sheep breeds in order to obtain better-quality wool. However, these breeding programs were unreliable, because at the time no one knew how to make the next generation inherit the desirable characteristics of the previous one.

Against this background, Mendel began his breeding experiments with pea plants. In early 1865, Mendel presented his results to a natural history society founded by his fellow monks in Brno. His results were published in 1866 as an article called "Experiments with Plant Hybrids." The paper made its way into scientific libraries in Europe and North America but aroused little interest. Mendel sent a copy to the famous Swiss botanist Karl Wilhelm von Nägeli, professor of botany at the University of Munich. Nägeli read the paper but apparently failed to appreciate the implications of the work.

In the mid-1800s, monasteries were often centers of education and learning where monks explored various aspects of the natural sciences.

Mendel Formulates His Laws

Mendel's study of inheritance revealed two general principles, now known as Mendel's Laws of Segregation and Independent Assortment. The Law of Segregation states that each inherited characteristic, or gene, is made up of two factors. One factor is derived from each parent. Today, these factors are called "alleles." For example, pea flowers may be purple or white, so there is an allele for purple flowers and an allele for white flowers. One allele is "dominant" and the other "recessive." In the case of pea flowers, purple is dominant and white is recessive. This can be written as capital P, meaning it is dominant, and lower-case w, meaning recessive. When two dominant alleles are present, the characteristic associated with the dominant allele will be inherited.

EXTENSION ACTIVITY

Weblink

The Mendel Museum in Brno

Analyze the article describing the museum dedicated to Gregor Mendel.

1. Gregor Mendel's scientific activity was developed in a monastery. Would his scientific achievements have been viewed differently during his lifetime, had he developed his research in a different context? Why? Propose some theories.
2. In what ways were Mendel's interest for botany and meteorology linked to each other? In your opinion, why was Mendel recognized only for his meteorologist activity in his lifetime?

Video

How Mendel Pea Plants helped us understand genetics

Assess the importance of Mendel's experiments with peas by watching this video.

1. What is the Punnett square? What is its use? Why might it have been designed in this way? Describe it in your own words.
2. What are the consequences of Mendel's studies for contemporary scientific research? What other applications might his studies have? Support your answer with examples.

Mendel chose to study pea plants because they grow and flower relatively quickly, enabling him to track changes between generations more easily.

If a dominant allele and a recessive allele are present, the characteristic associated with the dominant allele will still be the one passed on. For example, a pea plant with Pw or PP will have purple flowers. Only if both alleles are recessive, or ww, will the plant have white flowers.

The Law of Independent Assortment states that characteristics are inherited individually, not as packages. So, for example, whether peas are yellow or green or whether they are smooth or wrinkled in shape are inherited independently of each other. Peas can be smooth and yellow, wrinkled and yellow, smooth and green, or wrinkled and green.

A Missed Opportunity

About the same time as Mendel was experimenting with peas, the English naturalists Charles Darwin and Alfred Russel Wallace were separately working out the theory of evolution by natural selection. They had both noticed that all individuals vary slightly. They had also seen that, within a particular habitat–the natural home of an animal or plant–some variations give the individuals that possess them an advantage when it comes to **reproduction**.

The individuals that possess these advantages will survive in greater numbers than those that do not, and will pass them on to their offspring. Eventually individuals with these advantages become predominant in a society. This process is called “natural selection.” Darwin and Wallace showed that it is what drives the way animals and plants develop over time, or “evolve.” However, at the time neither Darwin nor Wallace knew how variation in species occurred. It was Mendel’s work on heredity that would help biologists understand how characteristics could be passed on from parents to their offspring. Mendel’s results were published a few years after Darwin’s *On the Origin of Species* (1859).

Mendel's work could have lent support to Darwin's theory of natural selection. A copy of Mendel's paper, written in German, was sent to Darwin. However, Darwin never read it.

Head of the Monastery

In 1868, Mendel was elected abbot of the monastery in Brünn. Although he remained interested in botany, meteorology, and bee-keeping, looking after the day-to-day running of the monastery left him little time for research or teaching. He died at Brünn on January 6, 1884.

Rediscovering Mendel's Work

Mendel's work had made little impact during his life. After his death, it was forgotten. It was rediscovered in 1900. At the time, three scientists were working independently on heredity, or the transmission of characteristics from one generation to another. They were the Dutch botanist Hugo de Vries, the German botanist Karl Erich Correns, and the Austrian botanist Erich Tschermak von Seysenegg.

William Bateson was influential in the development of the science of genetics in the early nineteenth century, based on Mendel's original research.

All three scientists came across copies of Mendel's paper on peas separately and drew attention to it. They published accounts of it within two months of each other. The British scientist William Bateson translated Mendel's paper into English. It was Bateson who introduced the term "genetics" to describe the science of heredity Mendel had founded.

CHROMOSOMES AND GENES

In 1879, the German biologist Walther Flemming had discovered tiny rod-shaped structures, later called chromosomes, in the **nucleus** of dividing cells. These chromosomes passed on what Mendel called heritable factors, or characteristics, to offspring. In the early 1900s, the U.S. biologist Thomas Hunt Morgan began studying the fruit fly (left). By 1911, he was convinced that the heritable factors were physical units named "genes." Morgan showed that genes were located at particular positions on the chromosomes, like beads on a necklace. Morgan produced a chromosome "map," showing the position of five genes. Scientists have now mapped hundreds of genes. They know that genes on the same chromosome are more likely to be inherited together than genes on different chromosomes, and that the closer they are on the chromosome the more likely they are to be inherited together. This "linkage" was also discovered by Morgan.

EXTENSION ACTIVITY

More

Karl Wilhelm von Nägeli (1817–1891)

Analyze the scientific career of Karl Wilhelm von Nägeli.

1. How could Nägeli make important scientific discoveries, such as his research on "transitory cytoblasts," while holding on to old ideas? In your opinion, was this attitude characteristic of the scientists of the past? Why or why not?
2. How could Nägeli discover the "transitory cytoblasts" without using modern scientific equipment? Formulate some theories.

Weblink

Darwin & Mendel's Afternoon Tea

Examine the fictional conversation between Charles Darwin and Gregor Mendel.

1. Compare and contrast the point of views expressed by the fictional Darwin and Mendel. How do they differ? In what do they agree?
2. How are Darwin's and Mendel's scientific discoveries related one to the other? Explain it in your own words.

RUBRIC

Write an Abstract

Students will use their library or *Google Scholar* to find a scientific research article or study related to penicillin, then write a 300-word abstract. An exemplary abstract will meet the following criteria.

- States the research question or problem that the author is answering
- Indicates the significance of the issue
- Describes and explains methods used by the scientist(s)
- Explains why the methods used by the scientist(s) were appropriate
- Explains why this article or study stands out and how it is different from others
- Clearly states how the article or study advances knowledge about the topic, why it is important, and how it can be used
- Introductory statement is clear, concise, and engaging
- Purpose is clear, concise, and relevant
- Explanation of the findings includes what was expected, discovered, accomplished, collected, and produced
- Clearly states the conclusion
- Conclusion describes how the work contributes to the field
- Writing is appropriate and free from grammatical errors

ALEXANDER FLEMING

1881–1955

Until the accidental discovery of penicillin by Scottish bacteriologist Alexander Fleming, people often died from infectious diseases or from infection following surgery. Fleming's work led to the development of bacteria-destroying chemicals called **antibiotics**.

Born in Lochfield, Scotland, on August 6, 1881, Alexander Fleming attended Kilmarnock Academy. In 1894, Fleming's father died and he moved to London and studied medicine. He graduated in 1906 and spent the rest of his career at St. Mary's Hospital, part of London University.

Bacteriology and Immunization

Fleming began working as a surgeon, but soon switched to bacteriology, which is the study of tiny bacteria present in water, soil, and the bodies of plants and animals. Some are harmless, or even beneficial, but others produce toxins, or poisons, that cause infection and disease. The German physician Robert Koch and French chemist Louis Pasteur had already isolated some disease-causing bacteria and developed vaccines to provide **immunization** against them. Immunization increases resistance to infection by stimulating the production of **antibodies**, part of the body's defense system. Antibodies are proteins made by white blood cells in response to the foreign molecules, or antigens, produced by disease-causing bacteria. They make the antigens harmless.

Somebody who has recovered from an infectious disease such as measles has natural immunity against future attacks because the antibodies remain in the blood stream. Immunization against a specific disease can be induced by introducing antibodies from an infected person or animal into the blood stream in order to stimulate the development of the antibodies to fight it. This process is known as vaccination or inoculation.

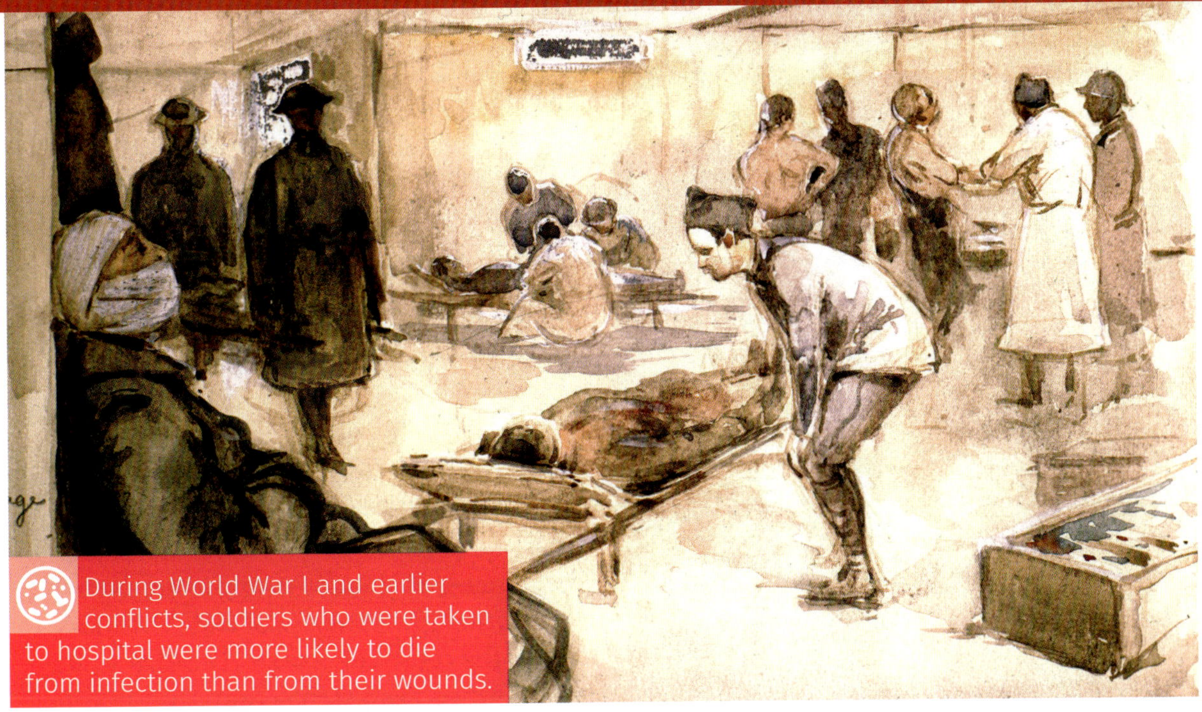

During World War I and earlier conflicts, soldiers who were taken to hospital were more likely to die from infection than from their wounds.

It was first used against smallpox in the 1700s. Immunization helped prevent the spread of diseases. But bacteriologists had yet to find a way to destroy bacteria-causing infection within the body. Several antibacterial agents, which kill bacteria, had been found by the early 1900s, but they all had harmful effects on human tissue.

Some Important Discoveries

Fleming served in the army medical corps in World War I (1914–1918). Many soldiers died from flesh wounds because doctors were unable to prevent bacterial infection from causing conditions such as septicemia, or blood poisoning. Fleming wanted to find a substance that destroyed harmful bacteria.

The first **recorded cure** using **penicillin** was on **November 25, 1930.**

In June 1942, the **United States** only had enough **penicillin** to treat **10 patients**.

The United States **produced** **2.3 million** doses of penicillin in time for the **D-Day landings** in 1944.

EXTENSION ACTIVITY

Document

"On the Antibacterial Action of Cultures of a Penicillium, with Special Reference to their Use in the Isolation of B. influenzæ"
Review Alexander Fleming's paper, published in the *Journal of Experimental Pathology* in 1929.

1. To which public is this paper addressed? How did Alexander Fleming describe his own discovery?
2. What are the main properties of penicillin, according to the summary of the article? What experiments did Fleming perform to prove the efficacy of penicillin?

Weblink

The Race to bring Penicillin to the Troops in WWII
Analyze the article describing the mass production of antibiotics during World War II.

1. Why might challenges have arose with the mass production of penicillin? Why did Howard Florey pursue his work on penicillin in the United States?
2. What actions did the U. S. authorities take to ensure penicillin's safety of use? Why? What might the consequences have been if these actions were not taken? Explain your response.

RUBRIC

Analyzing a Primary Source

Students will complete a thorough analysis of a primary source. An exemplary analysis will meet the following criteria.

- Identifies the creator of the source
- Explains what medium was used to create the primary source
- Describes why the source qualifies as a primary one
- Explores any literary devices used in the source
- Identifies the intended audience for the source
- Relates the creator's goals in creating the source
- Illustrates knowledge of the period and location in which the source was created
- Distinguishes between facts and opinions found in the source
- Examines the reliability of the source's creator
- Compares the source with similar documents
- Cites additional sources used in the analysis
- Presents information in a clear, concise manner
- Uses correct spelling, grammar, and punctuation

Alexander Fleming noticed while serving in World War I that antiseptics were of limited use against deep wounds that became infected.

After the war, Fleming investigated secretions of the body for their effects on bacteria. In 1922, he discovered lysozyme, an **enzyme** in tears and saliva. He showed that lysozyme has some bacteria-destroying power.

In 1928, Fleming, now professor of bacteriology at St. Mary's, made his most famous discovery. Some cultures he had left uncovered for a few days contained some specks of green mold on the agar gel. This was fairly common, but he also noticed that there was a bacteria-free circle around each speck of mold. The bacteria in the area around the mold had been killed. Fleming identified the mold as the fungus *Penicillium notatum*. When he exposed a number of disease-causing bacteria to the mold, he found that the mold killed some of them.

Fleming decided that the mold must be giving off a substance that was fatal to the bacteria, and he called this "penicillin." However, he failed to isolate the penicillin from the mold. He reported his findings to the *British Journal of Experimental Pathology* in 1929, but they aroused little interest. Fortunately, he kept a sample of his mold.

Drugs From Dyes

Meanwhile, the German biochemist Gerhard Domagk made a breakthrough. He was interested in the work of Paul Ehrlich, who had pioneered chemotherapy using dyes. Chemotherapy is the use of toxic chemicals to attack the causes of disease. Domagk tested various dyes against infections. In 1932, he found that a derivative of a dye called Prontosil red cured mice infected with streptococcal bacteria, which is responsible for diseases such as scarlet fever. The active chemical in the drug was called sulfanilamide. Two more chemicals, produced in 1938 and 1940, proved effective against pneumonia. A third in 1941 was successful in treating the brain infection meningitis. Known as sulfa drugs, they saved many lives in their early years of use.

A Valuable Powder

In 1935, pathologist Howard Florey and biochemist Ernst Chain began researching antibacterial substances to control wound infection. In 1938, after Chain came across Fleming's observations of the behavior of the *Penicillium notatum* mold, he and Florey tried to isolate the substance. After a long and difficult effort, they extracted some penicillin in the form of a yellow powder. They found that a solution of one part of the yellow powder in a million parts of a solvent prevented the growth of lethal bacteria in mice. Then, they tested it on a human subject.

Their first patient, although recovering, died when they ran out of penicillin. But penicillin had proved its effectiveness. The problem was maintaining a supply, but production sped up after the United States entered World War II in 1941.

Continuing the Work

After his discovery of penicillin, Fleming went on to do other important work, identifying the organisms that infect wounds and developing new techniques for staining bacteria. He studied the effects of various disinfectants on different bacterial species and showed how streptococcal cross-infections can occur in hospitals. In the 1960s, Chain went on to discover penicillinase, an enzyme that some bacteria can learn to synthesize, which makes them resistant to penicillin. Alexander Fleming and Howard Florey were knighted for the part they had played in developing penicillin, and in 1945 Alexander Fleming, Howard Florey, and Ernst Chain shared the Nobel Prize for Physiology or Medicine. Fleming retired in 1954.

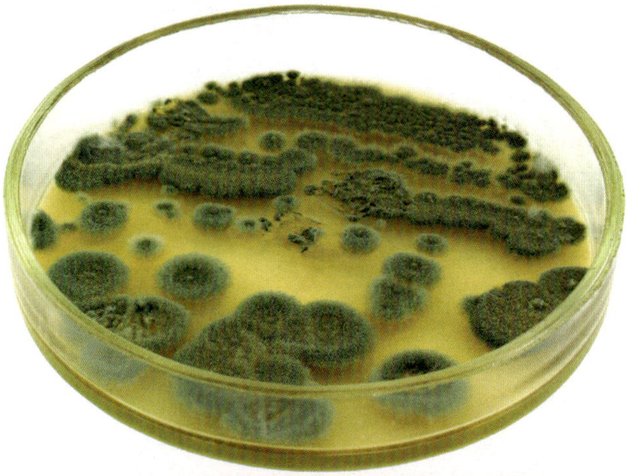

The penicillin mold that grew in Fleming's petri dish killed bacteria, but it could not be used in medicine until its active ingredients had been isolated.

Although Florey and Chain had been responsible for penicillin's transformation into a usable drug, it was Fleming who had become identified in the public mind with its creation, resulting in the "Fleming myth," as he himself called it. After his death on March 11, 1955, Fleming was buried in St. Paul's Cathedral, London.

ERNST BORIS CHAIN (1906–1979)

British biochemist Ernst Chain (right) was born in Berlin, Germany. He graduated in chemistry and physiology from the Friedrich Wilhelm Institute, and then worked at the Institute of Pathology, Charité Hospital, Berlin from 1930 to 1933. The anti-Jewish policies of Germany's Adolf Hitler forced Chain to flee to England. There, he worked at Cambridge University before joining Howard Florey at Oxford University in 1935. They isolated penicillin and demonstrated its unique antibacterial properties. After the war, Chain shared the 1945 Nobel Prize for Physiology or Medicine with Florey and Fleming. He then became director of the International Research Center for Chemical Microbiology. In 1954, he helped the U.S. pharmaceutical company the Beecham Group to develop a range of semi-synthetic penicillins. In 1961, Chain returned to England to become professor of **biochemistry** at Imperial College, University of London. He held various posts there until 1979. He died in Ireland the same year.

EXTENSION ACTIVITY

First Hand

Sir Alexander Fleming – Banquet Speech

Examine the transcription of the speech Alexander Fleming gave at the reception for his Nobel Prize in 1945.

1. How does Alexander Fleming describe his own discovery? How does this description differ from the one in Fleming's 1929 paper? Why might these two descriptions differ?
2. Do you agree with Fleming's statement about team work? Is team work still necessary in the development of scientific research? Why or why not?

Weblink

First step in saving millions of lives

Examine the scientific achievements of Howard Florey.

1. What was the contribution of Florey to the development of penicillin? Describe it in your own words.
2. Why was patenting a drug was considered medically unethical in Florey's times? In your opinion, why is patenting a drug no longer considered unethical today? What are the advantages and disadvantages of drug patents? Formulate some hypotheses.

RUBRIC

Analyzing a Scientific Biography

Students will research the life of a scientific figure and present their findings. An exemplary biographical analysis will meet the following criteria.

- Illustrates strong knowledge of the subject
- Identifies the author of the biography
- Describes why the subject of the biography is important
- Contains information about the time and place in which the subject was born
- Lists important events in the subject's life
- Explains how events in the subject's life impacted him or her
- Makes inferences about the subject, based on events in his or her life
- Explains how the subject influenced the world while he or she lived
- Researches the cultural and historical context of the subject's life
- Examines the effect that the subject has had on the modern world
- Supplements information from the biography with independent research
- Organizes the analysis in a logical, effective manner
- Uses correct spelling, grammar, and punctuation
- Cites all sources used in the analysis

THE LEAKEYS

Louis 1903–1972, Mary 1913–1996

Much of what is known about early humans comes from the Leakeys' work. Their work suggested that human evolution began in Africa, not in Asia as was previously thought. They also showed that humans had existed for much longer than previously believed.

Louis Seymour Bazett Leakey was born on August 7, 1903, in Kabete, Kenya. In 1922, he went to Cambridge University, where he studied archeology and anthropology, which is the study of humans and their culture. Louis graduated in 1926, and returned to Africa, where he met his first wife, Frida Avern. In 1930, Louis was awarded a PhD. from Cambridge University.

Leakey worked in Olduvai Gorge in Tanzania before returning to England in 1933. There he met Mary Nicol. She was born in London on February 6, 1913.

Louis and Mary Leakey worked closely together. When Mary found the Zinjanthropus skull, for example, it was Louis who dug it out of the rock.

Louis and Mary shared a fascination with archaeology and anthropology, and became close. Frida Leakey filed for divorce, and in 1936 Louis and Mary married. They later had three sons, Jonathan, Richard, and Philip. In 1937, Louis and Mary returned to Olduvai Gorge. Louis studied the Kikuyu people and Mary excavated a late Stone Age site. There she found primitive tools, burial mounds, and traces of dwellings. The Leakeys' explorations in the Rift Valley yielded stone tools in the form of hand axes and hammer stones.

Ancestors of Humans

The tools had been made by a hominid called *Homo erectus*, or "upright man." Hominids are a type of mammal called primates, of which humans are the only surviving species. Hominids include the ancestors of modern humans. At this time, most people believed that *Homo erectus* was the earliest hominid.

The Leakeys spent nearly all of their careers working in the Olduvai Gorge in Tanzania. The gorge is part of the Great Rift Valley of East Africa.

The first *Homo erectus* fossil was found in Java, Asia, by Eugene Dubois in 1891. It was dated to about 500,000 years ago. The study of fossils remains is called paleontology. Most paleontologists at the time believed that Asia was where the human line split from the other apes. Then, in 1924, the South African anatomist Raymond Dart found a hominid skull he named *Australopithecus africanus*. Dart's assertion that this was a stage between apes and humans provoked controversy. Later discoveries suggested that he was correct. These Australopithecines were a genus of hominids. Carbon dating shows they lived between 4.4 million and 1 million years ago.

More Finds

In 1959, in Olduvai Gorge, Mary discovered the skull of another human ancestor. Louis allocated it to a new genus, Zinjanthropus, but it is now called *Australopithecus boisei*. The following year the Leakeys discovered the remains of the skull and hand bones of a species Louis classified as *Homo habilis* meaning "Handy Man." The remains were 1.7 million years old. This was clearly a species that had existed between Australopithecines and *Homo erectus*.

EXTENSION ACTIVITY

Document

"Mary Leakey: Unearthing History."
Examine the profile of Mary Leakey published by *Scientific American* in October, 1994.

1. How did Mary Leakey's personal life and experience influence her scientific research? In your opinion, was Leakey an exceptional case, or are all researchers influenced by their personal experiences? Justify your answer.
2. What is the scientific importance of Laetoli's footprints today? Why might some scientists accuse Leakey of forging one of the footprints? If true, what reasons might Leakey have had for doing it?

Weblink

Ngorongoro Conservation Area
Analyze the UNESCO webpage dedicated to the Ngorongoro Conservation Area.

1. Why did the UNESCO add the Ngorongoro Conservation Area to its World Heritage List? How did the Leakey's discovery contribute to the UNESCO choice?
2. What possible dangers are there for the fossil remains in the Ngorongoro Conservation area? What action does the UNESCO suggest to protect the fossil remains? Will these actions be effective? Why or why not? What other actions could be taken to this effect?

RUBRIC

Analyzing a Scientific Video

Students will watch and assess a video related to a scientific discovery, and write an analysis of the video. An exemplary video analysis will meet the following criteria.

- Identifies the purpose of the video
- Identifies the intended audience of the video
- Identifies the video as a primary or secondary source
- Discusses the scientific and social context of the video
- Describes how the content of the video is presented
- Summarizes the information and opinions presented in the video
- Analyzes the quality of the content presented in the video
- Assesses the effectiveness of the video
- Determines whether the images and graphics used in the video relate to the content
- Determines whether the video is easy to follow and understand
- Gives the analysis a clear and consistent purpose
- Organizes the analysis in a logical, effective manner
- Presents a strong, clear argument about the video
- Provides strong and accurate details to support the argument about the video
- Considers other perspectives on the purpose and effectiveness of the video
- Cites all sources used in the analysis

Richard Leakey followed his parents and became a leading expert on the evolution of hominids.

Footprints from Long Ago

In 1974, American paleoanthropologist Donald Johanson discovered a partial female skeleton of *Australopithecus afarensis* in Ethiopia. This was a type of Australopithecines from which humans may have evolved that lived from 3.9 to 3.0 million years ago. Believed to be about 3.5 million years old, the fossil was nicknamed "Lucy."

In 1978, at Laetoli, near Olduvai, Mary Leakey and her team discovered hominid footprints. Two individuals had walked side by side through volcanic ash nearly 3.7 million years ago. Their trail was immediately covered by fresh deposits. A third, perhaps a child, had trodden in the footsteps of the larger individual. The footprints are likely those of *Australopithecus afarensis*, the species to which Lucy belonged. The footprints were firm evidence that early hominids walked on two legs. Soon after, Mary left Laetoli to tour, lecture, and raise funds. Her autobiography, *Disclosing the Past*, was published in 1984.

Richard Leakey

Richard Erskine Frere Leakey was born at Nairobi on December 19, 1944. At first he did not want to become a paleontologist, and so he became a safari guide, while also catching wild animals for zoos. In 1963, while he was leading an expedition in the area around Lake Natron in Tanzania, Richard found an Australopithecine jaw. The discovery made him determined to become a paleontologist. In 1965, he went to London and caught up on two years of missed high school in six months, after which he returned to Africa and worked with his father on excavations.

More Human Ancestors Revealed

In 1968, Richard Leakey became director of the National Museum of Kenya. He began excavating at Koobi Fora on Lake Turkana, then called Lake Rudolf, which became one of the richest sources of early hominid fossils and stone tools in Africa. Starting in 1969, Leakey and his team found about 400 fossil bones from about 230 individual hominids.

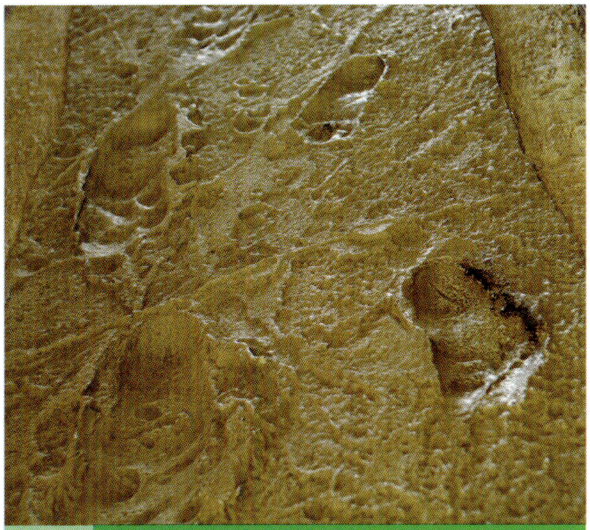

At Olduvai Gorge, the Leakeys found not only bones and ancient stone tools. There were also fossilized footprints that had been left by early hominids.

The finds included part of an early Homo skull, discovered in 1972, which may be 2 million years old. Another sensational find was "Turkana Boy," the most complete skeleton of an early hominid yet known. The fossil, discovered in 1984, is about 1.5 million years old, and is classed as *Homo ergaster*. In 1970, Richard married Meave Epps, also a paleontologist and primatologist. In 1992, she found a new species, *Australopithecus anamensis*. This was followed in 2001 by the discovery of a fossil between 3.5 and 3.2 million years old. Named *Kenyanthropus platyops*, its cheek bones and flat face resembled those of a modern human.

During the 1980s, Richard spent more time on wildlife conservation, directing the Kenya Wildlife Service. He battled corruption in Kenya but found it impossible to achieve his goals, and in the 2000s, became professor of anthropology at Stony Brook University, New York. Today, his daughter, Louise, manages her own paleontological excavations.

THE STORY OF HUMAN DEVELOPMENT

The story of early human development can be traced through the study of the tools used by the first hominids. Mary Leakey contributed much to the picture with her analysis of the large collections of stone tools the Leakeys discovered in the lowest layers of the Olduvai Gorge. The tools, which dated to between 1.9 and 1.5 million years ago, had been made by using a smooth pebble as a hammer in order to chip small, sharp-edged flakes off another rock or pebble. These flakes could be used for cutting and scraping. The tools Mary Leakey found at Olduvai were made by early species of Homo. They were used to cut meat off animals that were already dead and to scrape flesh from animal hides.

About 1.4 million years ago, larger, more highly fashioned hand axes and cleavers began to be made. They are called Acheulean for St. Acheul, France, where they were first identified. These tools were made by Homo erectus, who began to migrate from Africa about 1 million years ago. Scientists believe Acheulean tools, found in Africa, the Near East, and Europe, were in use until about 200,000 years ago.

EXTENSION ACTIVITY

Video

Human Ancestor 'Lucy' Was a Tree-Climber

Analyze the latest scientific findings relating to Lucy.

1. Why are Lucy's fossil remains still studied 40 years after their discovery? Which scientific techniques have been recently employed to study Lucy's fossil bones? Why?
2. Why is the information obtained using these modern techniques important for modern scientific research on human evolution? What other information could Lucy's bones reveal? Formulate some hypotheses.

Weblink

Human Evolution Timeline Interactive

Explore the milestones of the human evolution by reviewing this timeline.

1. Why does the timeline include information on climate fluctuation? Compare and contrast the human evolution milestones and the climate fluctuation as shown by the timeline. What conclusions can be drawn from this?
2. Why did the length of time between human evolution milestones decrease over time? Discuss some possible reasons.

MELVIN CALVIN

1911–1997

Photosynthesis is the process by which green plants and bacteria use the energy of sunlight to make sugar molecules and oxygen from water and carbon dioxide. The details of photosynthesis were first explained by Melvin Calvin. The process is vital for all life forms.

Melvin Calvin, the son of Russian parents who had emigrated to the United States, was born in St. Paul, Minnesota, on April 8, 1911. He graduated in chemistry in 1931, and received a PhD. in the same subject four years later from the University of Minnesota. From 1935 until 1937 he carried out research at the University of Manchester, England, before being invited by the physical chemist Gilbert Lewis to become an instructor at the University of California at Berkeley.

Lewis introduced Calvin to the physicist Ernest Lawrence, winner of the 1939 Nobel Prize in Physics, and director of the Radiation Laboratory at Berkeley. Apart from two years during World War II (1941–1945), when he worked on the Manhattan Project at Los Alamos, New Mexico, Calvin remained at Berkeley for the rest of his career. His early research was on the study of organic molecules. A molecule consists of atoms linked by chemical bonds. "Organic" compounds are those that contain carbon. These compounds form the basic material from which all living tissue is made.

Carbon-14 Isotopes

In 1931, Lawrence invented the cyclotron, a device that accelerates charged subatomic particles such as electrons, protons, and nuclei to high levels of energy. In 1940, U.S. physicists used the cyclotron to produce isotopes of radioactive carbon-14. Isotopes are atoms of an element that have the same number of positively charged protons in the nucleus but different numbers of neutrons, which carry no charge.

Most elements are made up of a mixture of stable isotopes. This means they do not decompose readily. A few have naturally occurring radioactive isotopes. Carbon-14, or 14C, is a radioactive carbon isotope produced by the impact of cosmic rays, or charged particles, on nitrogen atoms in the atmosphere. The carbon-14 isotope can also be produced artificially by exposing stable carbon isotopes to radiation in an accelerator. Chemically and biologically, radioisotopes behave in similar ways to stable isotopes. Their radiation can be easily monitored, so they can be used to "label" particular atoms or groups when studying chemical reactions and biological processes.

Ernest Lawrence was awarded the Nobel Prize in Physics for his invention of the cyclotron. It was the most powerful particle accelerator in use in the 1930s and 1940s.

Photosynthesis Revealed

In 1946, Lawrence suggested that Calvin work with carbon-14 isotopes. Calvin became director of the Radiation Laboratory's Biological Division. In 1949, he began studying the chemical reactions that make up photosynthesis, the process by which plants turn sunlight into energy. Scientists knew that photosynthesis occurs in two stages, then called the "light" and "dark" stages. The stages are now called "light-dependent" and "light-independent." In the light stage, a plant "captures" energy from sunlight. In the dark stage, which carries on without light, carbon dioxide combines with water to form organic compounds.

The earliest fossils of organisms that used **photosynthesis** are **3.4 billion years old.**

A typical **plant cell** holds **10-100 chloroplasts, or bag-like structures.**

The cells in the **interior tissues** of a leaf contain between **450,000 and 800,000 chloroplasts** for every fraction of a square inch of leaf.

EXTENSION ACTIVITY

More

Photosynthesis

Evaluate the importance of the photosynthesis process.

1. Why is photosynthesis important for all living creatures? Explain the process of photosynthesis in your own words. How are most living creatures linked to photosynthesis? Support your answer with examples.
2. Why might "black smokers" bacteria and the creatures feeding off them be the only living creatures that do not obtain their energy from photosynthesis? Develop possible hypotheses.

Weblink

A Brief Historical Review of the Invention of the Cyclotron

Examine the article describing the invention of the cyclotron.

1. How does a cyclotron work? Explain it in your own words.
2. How might Ernest Lawrence have come to his idea for the invention of the cyclotron? Can you think of any other scientific discovery with a similar origin? Support your answer with examples.

These organic compounds are called carbohydrates. They include sugars such as glucose, for example. Carbohydrates are stored in roots and leaves and give the plant energy for growth and other living processes.

Calvin used carbon-14 to trace the movement of carbon through the reactions that convert carbon dioxide to sugars. In 1957, he described the principal steps in what is now often called "the Calvin cycle." Calvin also discovered that it is the action of sunlight on chlorophyll that drives photosynthesis.

Chlorophyll is the green coloring matter in plants and leaves that absorbs light energy. Plants can convert sunlight to food because their leaf cells contain structures called chloroplasts, which are like small bags.

Each chloroplast contains many other tiny, flattened membranes called thylakoids. The surfaces of the thylakoids are covered with chlorophyll, the green pigment that absorbs light energy in plants. A pigment has a special structure that lets it absorb light of a particular color. The color of light is determined by its wavelength. Chlorophyll absorbs light of red and blue-violet, so these wavelengths are likely the ones most helpful for photosynthesis.

The remainder of the light is reflected back by the chlorophyll. Without red and blue-violet wavelengths, the light is mainly green, giving chlorophyll its color. Chlorophyll absorbs light and releases electrons when it does so. It is these electrons that drive the chemical reactions of photosynthesis.

The leaves of plants absorb carbon dioxide and release oxygen. This makes them vital to maintaining the balance of gases in Earth's atmosphere.

THE STRUCTURE OF A LEAF

A waxy cuticle protects the upper surface, or epidermis, of the leaf. Beneath the epidermis is a layer of palisade cells that absorbs light. Beneath the palisade layer is a spongy layer full of air spaces where carbon dioxide can circulate. The exchange of carbon dioxide and oxygen takes place in the stoma. Water is drawn into the leaf by xylem cells in veins that reach to the plant's roots. Phloem cells carry food from the leaves to the rest of the plant.

"Lollipops" Provide the Answer

Calvin identified the steps in the Calvin cycle using an apparatus resembling a "lollipop." This consisted of a spherical flask mounted above a smaller flask. The complete apparatus was a series of such "lollipops." The large flask contained a "suspension," or mixture, of water, plant nutrient, and an algae named chlorella. Algae are plants that have chlorophyll and other pigments but do not have stems, roots, or leaves. The group includes seaweeds.

The suspension was poured in through the tube at the top, and air entered through another tube on the side. The carbon dioxide in the air was traced using carbon-14. The larger flask was exposed to bright light. The smaller flask contained methanol, or methyl alcohol, that was kept gently boiling. Supplied with light, water, and carbon dioxide, the algae carried out photosynthesis. At different intervals, a valve at the bottom of the flask was opened, allowing a small amount of the suspension to enter the tube.

The boiling methanol and the heat quickly stopped the photosynthetic reactions of the algae. By tapping first one "lollipop" and then another, it was possible to stop photosynthesis at different stages for study. Compounds that had formed could be isolated by tracing the carbon they contained using carbon-14. This allowed Calvin to follow each of the steps by which glucose is produced during the light-independent stage of photosynthesis. Calvin began his experiments in 1949. He published his results in a book entitled *The Path of Carbon in Photosynthesis* in 1957.

Honored for his Achievements

Calvin received many awards and honors for his work on photosynthesis. He was awarded the Nobel Prize in Chemistry in 1961 and the U.S. National Medal of Science in 1989. Later, Calvin turned his attention to the possibility of using photosynthesis in oil-producing plants to produce fuel substitutes. He was also interested in the chemical evolution of life, especially the part that photosynthesis may have played in this process.

EXTENSION ACTIVITY

Transparency–Chart

Paper Chromatography

Analyze the method used by Melvin Calvin to identify the products produced during the various stages of photosynthesis.

1. How does paper chromatography work? Explain the process in your own words. Why did Melvin Calvin use paper chromatography for identifying the products formed at different stages of the photosynthesis process?
2. What are other possible uses and applications of paper chromatography? Formulate some hypotheses, then research in the library and online for other actual applications of this method.

Weblink

My hero: Melvin Calvin

Examine a blog article relating an anecdote about Melvin Calvin.

1. Did the author ever meet Calvin in person? Who are the sources of the anecdote he reports? Does this make it more or less trustworthy? Why?
2. How does this anecdote relate the idea of a "stereotypical mad scientist" mentioned in the article? What does such anecdote suggest about Calvin as a person?

CRICK, FRANKLIN, AND WATSON

1916–2004 (Crick), 1920–1958 (Franklin), 1928– (Watson)

The work of Rosalind Franklin, Francis Crick, and James D. Watson led to the discovery of **deoxyribonucleic acid**, or **DNA**. DNA makes up genes, the units of heredity. This discovery underpins all modern understanding of genetics.

Rosalind Franklin was born in London on July 25, 1920. She graduated in chemistry and physics in 1941, and in 1942 she joined the British Coal Utilization Research Association to help the war effort. In 1947, Franklin moved to Paris to work at the Central Government Laboratory for Chemistry. There, she learned the techniques of x-ray diffraction, or x-ray crystallography. These would prove vital in the search for the structure of the DNA molecule. A crystal is an arrangement of regularly spaced atoms. If x-rays pass through a crystal, each of the atoms in the crystal bends the x-ray beam in a characteristic way caused by the density of electrons in each atom. Electrons are particles with negative charge that surround each atom's nucleus.

Molecules are far too small to examine under a microscope, but x-ray crystallography can reveal a molecule's shape. X-rays expose photographic film, so if a piece of film is placed behind the crystal, the deflected x-rays form a pattern of spots that appear when the film is developed. The pattern reveals the density of the electrons in each part of the picture. Knowing the electron density allows scientists to calculate the position of each atom in the crystal. This can be plotted as a computer graphic or used to build a model.

In 1951, Franklin became a research associate in the biophysics research laboratory at King's College, London. There she met Maurice Wilkins, assistant director of the laboratory. Franklin and Wilkins were both set to work on examining the DNA molecule.

Hunting for DNA

In the 1890s, the German zoologist August Friedrich Leopold Weismann had proposed that every living organism contains "germ plasm." He suggested that this substance controls the development of every part of the body and is passed from parents to offspring. Weismann also realized that, if germ plasm from both parents is mixed at fertilization, the amount of it would increase from one generation to the next. Since this does not happen, there must be some form of cell division in which the resulting cells receive only half the full amount of germ plasm. This reduction division process is called meiosis.

In 1946, it was found that Weismann's "germ plasm" is made from a nucleic acid called deoxyribonucleic acid, or DNA. Franklin designed a camera that provided images of DNA that had been stretched into a thin fiber. She was the first to report that the sugar-phosphate backbone of DNA lies on the outside of the DNA molecule. Her x-rays showed that DNA might be arranged as a helix. A helix is a spiral shape, like the thread on a screw.

Making the Double Helix

Franklin was close to discovering the structure of DNA, but two other people would prove vital to the outcome. Francis Harry Crick was born on June 8, 1916, in England. In 1937, he graduated with a degree in physics from University College, London. In 1949, he joined the Medical Research Council unit at the Cavendish Laboratory, Cambridge, where he studied x-ray diffraction of proteins. James Dewey Watson was born on April 6, 1928, in Chicago, Illinois. He graduated in **zoology** at Chicago University in 1947. His interest in the huge range of diversity of birds led him to study genetics.

Since the Cavendish Laboratory opened as part of Cambridge University in 1874, it has been a leading center of experimental physics.

Watson became convinced that the chemical structure of genes was of fundamental importance. He began investigating the structure of nucleic acids and proteins, and learned that scientists were using x-ray diffraction patterns of protein crystals to study protein molecule structure. In 1951, he moved to the Cavendish Laboratory, Cambridge. There he began working with Francis Crick on the problem of the structure of DNA.

Maurice Wilkins showed Crick and Watson Franklin's photographs of the x-ray diffraction patterns made by DNA crystals. Crick and Watson believed that, if the structure of DNA were known, its role in heredity would become clear. Helped by Franklin's diffraction studies, they made a model of DNA based on its known properties.

EXTENSION ACTIVITY

Video

Celebrating Crystallography – an Animated Adventure
Review the origin and uses of x-ray crystallography by watching the video.

1. How does structural analysis work? What are its uses?
2. How has scientific research benefited from structural analysis and x-ray crystallography? What do these two kinds of research have in common? In what ways are they different? Provide evidence for your explanation.

Weblink

Unraveling the double helix
Analyze the ideas that led to the discovery of DNA chemical structure.

1. How did Crick and Watson discover the structure of DNA? Were their methods effective? Why or why not? What was the contribution of other scientists to this discovery?
2. According to the article, what other discoveries ensued from Crick's and Watson's work on the DNA double helix? What was the contribution of different scientific disciplines to these discoveries?

The structure of DNA is like a twisting ladder. The rungs can divide, allowing the outer strands to divide and recombine.

Crick and Watson realized that the DNA molecule must be arranged in a double spiral. This so-called double helix was like two long twisting ladders wound around each other. Eventually, Crick and Watson were able to show how a molecule consisting of two helices running in opposite directions could separate into single strands and how each strand could then assemble a complementary strand. They described their findings in two papers published in the British scientific journal *Nature* in April and May, 1953.

Crick, Watson, and Wilkins received the Nobel Prize in Physiology or Medicine in 1962 for their work on DNA. Rosalind Franklin had died of cancer in 1958. Nobel Prizes are not awarded posthumously, so she did not share in the award.

DNA Structure

The discovery of the structure of DNA has been described as the key to the scientific understanding the chemistry of reproduction. Chemical analysis had already shown that DNA is a polymer, or a long, repeating chain made up of a backbone of sugar and phosphate atoms. Four nitrogen-containing, or nitrogenous, bases are attached to the sugar. These are cytosines, thymine, adenine, and guanine. Crick and Watson found that the bases link to each other in a particular way. Cytosine and guanine link together, and thymine and adenine link together.

The double helix means that DNA's structure is formed by two long molecules twisted around one another. The sugar-phosphate backbone is on the outside of the helix and the bases are on the inside. DNA is contained in chromosomes in the nucleus of every cell. When a cell splits into two, its DNA is copied so that each of the new cells has its own DNA and the DNA is identical in both cells. First, the double helix straightens out. Untwisted, the DNA is shaped like a ladder. The sugar-phosphate molecules form the sides of the ladder and the bases form the rungs.

RUBRIC

Analyzing a Scientific Blog

Students will complete a thorough analysis of a blog that explores scientific topics or events. An exemplary analysis will meet the following criteria.

- Chooses a relevant and meaningful blog
- Provides a working link to the blog
- Identifies the blogger
- Presents information about the blogger
- Assesses the blogger's reliability
- Considers and assesses the blogger's perspective
- Determines the blogger's intended audience
- Determines whether the blogger had first hand knowledge of the topic or event, or whether he or she is reporting as a secondary source
- Summarizes the topic or event that the blogger is covering
- Determines any bias present in the blog postings
- Examines and evaluates any content tags used by the blogger
- Uses additional sources to confirm any claims made by the blog
- Uses correct spelling, grammar, and punctuation

The DNA molecule gradually splits in two. The pairs of bases separate and the two strands part. Each strand has a row of the four different types of single bases joined to it, which will only bond with their appropriate opposite numbers. More sugar and phosphate groups join the bases to make a new backbone. Each single strand has assembled its own partner, making the two double strands identical. The nitrogenous bases of DNA instruct the cell to make protein molecules. Some of these are used to build or repair the cell, some help with the chemical reactions that keep the cell working, and some turn genes on or off. Such molecules, for example, activate genes governing sexual maturity when humans reach puberty.

Genetic Engineering

When bacteria defend themselves against attack by viruses, called bacteriophages, they use enzymes to cut the bacteriophage DNA at specific points in its chain. These "restriction enzymes" gave scientists the idea for a way to retrieve sections of DNA. This DNA could then be stored, transferred, or rearranged between organisms. This process is called **genetic engineering**. Genetic engineering opened the way to many developments. Biochemists can now produce genetically modified, or GM, crops, for example, in which the gene that makes one species resistant to a particular pest or disease can be transferred to another species. In medicine, genetic engineering can be used to combat a number of genetically acquired diseases by altering the genes responsible for passing on the disease.

Francis Crick died in 2004. James Watson was forced to resign his academic posts in 2008, after making controversial public comments. In order to raise money, he sold his Nobel Prize medal in 2014.

DUPLICATING DNA

When a DNA molecule reproduces itself, it slowly unravels, and the single bases link to their relevant opposite numbers. Eventually, more sugar and phosphate groups join the bases, creating a new backbone. The process makes a pair of identical DNA molecules.

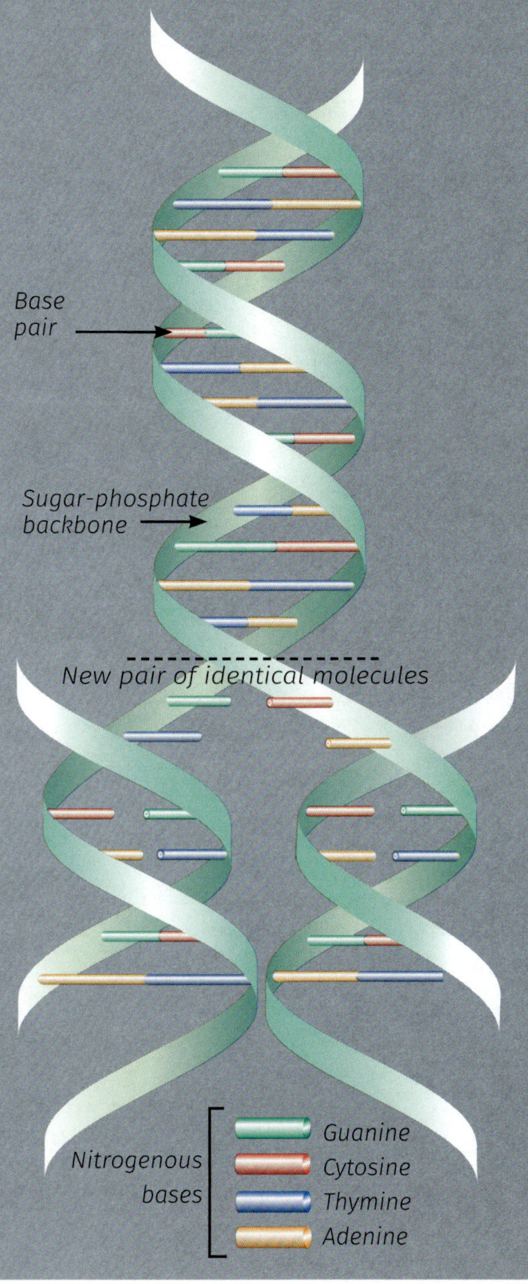

EXTENSION ACTIVITY

More

Genetic Fingerprinting

Asses the importance of genetic fingerprinting and its possible uses.

1. What are the pros of genetic fingerprinting? Why would some people support the use of DNA testing? What factors would cause these people to support it?
2. What are the cons of genetic fingerprinting? Why would some people oppose the use of DNA testing? What factors would cause these people to be against it?
3. Are these arguments based on fact, opinion, or both? Support your answer with examples.

Weblink

The Guardian view on genetics: engineer, but with ethics

Analyze the article about ethical implications of DNA manipulation.

1. According to the author, what could the danger of genetic manipulation be? Why could the genetic manipulation be seen as a possible threat?
2. What advantages could there be to using genetic manipulation? What possible solutions are there to the threats posed by this technology?
3. In your opinion, is the possibility of causing the extinction of some species of mosquitoes through genetic manipulation ethical? Why or why not? Justify your answer.

RUBRIC

Creating a Timeline

Students will explore a topic related to a scientific event and create a timeline to present their research on scientific events connected to this topic. An exemplary timeline will meet the following criteria.

- Includes the most significant events pertaining to the topic to be compared and analyzed
- Includes interesting events
- Uses accurate information for all events, including date, location, and major details
- Orders the events in a chronological sequence
- Describes each event with accurate, vivid, and specific details
- Presents the topic from three or more perspectives
- Inspires the reader to ask thoughtful questions regarding the events and perspectives presented in the timeline
- Uses correct spelling, grammar, and punctuation
- Presents the timeline in a visually attractive and striking manner
- Presents the timeline in a neat, organized manner that is logical and easy to follow
- Uses creativity to present the timeline in an engaging manner
- Effectively communicates historical information relating to the topic
- Supports each event with reliable sources
- Includes a correctly formatted bibliography of all sources used to create the timeline

Timeline of Scientific Breakthroughs

The history of the life sciences has been marked by important breakthroughs. Scientists have, slowly but surely, pieced together information about the nature of life. They have learned how life forms evolve and how tiny life forms can have great effects. Above all, scientists have found that humans are an important part of the living world.

c.330 BC

Aristotle suggests the idea that humans are at the top of a "great chain of being."

1735

Linnaeus publishes *Systema Naturae*. The work introduces a two-word description for all plants and animals. Linnaeus divides all species into three kingdoms.

1795

James Hutton claims that Earth is far older than previously thought. Earlier estimates had been that Earth was only about 4,000 years old.

1858

Alfred Russel Wallace describes evolution by natural selection to Charles Darwin, who publishes his own work on the subject in 1859.

1856

Louis Pasteur invents a way to kill microorganisms in milk and other liquids by heating them. His research proved the germ theory of disease.

1863

Gregor Mendel studies pea plants and comes up with two laws of inheritance that include the idea of dominant and recessive traits.

1953

Francis Crick and James Watson publish their discovery of the DNA molecule as a double helix.

2003

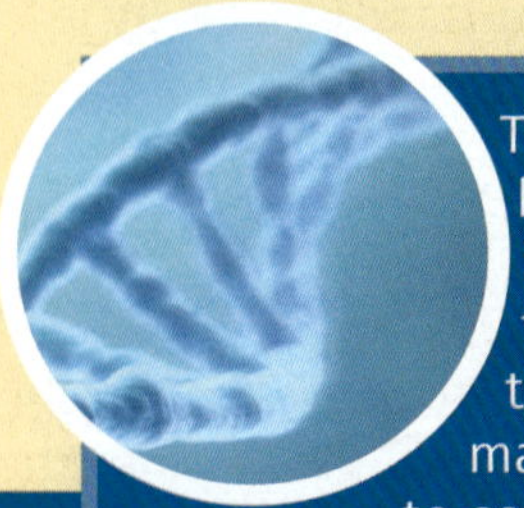

The whole human genome is sequenced for the first time. This makes it easier to combat genetic disorders by altering DNA.

Quiz

1 Carolus Linnaeus devised his system of classifying plants and animals after an expedition to which region in 1732?

2 Edward Jenner found he could stop people from getting smallpox by vaccinating them with what other disease?

3 What was the name of the ship on which naturalist Charles Darwin sailed around the world in the 1830s?

4 Louis Pasteur stopped contamination of beer and wine by using which method to kill harmful yeasts?

5 What disease passed on in the saliva of infected dogs did Louis Pasteur manage to cure by inoculation?

6 Gregor Mendl discovered the basic laws of heredity by experimenting with which plants?

7 Alexander Fleming discovered that penicillin was an antiseptic almost by accident. What type of organism is penicillin?

8 Which radioactive isotope did Melvin Calvin use to investigate the dark phase of photosynthesis?

9 What technique enabled Rosalind Franklin to create images that suggested the structure of DNA?

10 What is the term for the artificial altering of the sequence of DNA in an organism, either by inserting or removing cells?

ANSWERS
1. Lapland 2. Cowpox
3. The HMS *Beagle* 4. He heated the liquids and then sealed their containers 5. Rabies 6. Pea plants 7. Penicillin is a mold
8. Carbon-14 9. x-ray diffraction or x-ray crystallography
10. Genetic engineering

EXTENSION ACTIVITY

Transparency–Timeline

Timeline of Scientific Breakthroughs

Analyze important events and discoveries in the field of life sciences in different cultural, historical, and contemporary contexts.

1. Why might these events be featured in the timeline? What makes these events important or significant?
2. How might people from different social or ideological groups have interpreted these events when they took place? How might their opinions differ from those of people in the same social or ideological groups today? Why?
3. What effects did one of these scientific breakthroughs have on modern science?
4. How might these events have shaped the world today? Explain your response with evidence found on the internet or at the library.
5. How might recent events affect the way people interpret these past events?

Key Words

antibiotics: substances that kill or prevent the growth of other microorganisms

antibodies: defense proteins made by white cells in the body to counter invading proteins known as antigens

antiseptics: substances that prevent the growth or spread of microorganisms

bacteria: single-celled microorganisms that can cause disease

biochemistry: the study of substances in living organisms and the chemical reactions in which they are involved

biology: the study of living things. Biology has many branches, such as botany, genetics, and zoology.

cells: the units of living matter from which almost all organisms are built

deoxyribonucleic acid (DNA): a molecule that forms the basis of genetic inheritance in living organisms

enzyme: a protein that speeds up chemical reactions in the body

evolution: the process by which organisms change over long periods of time

fermentation: the breakdown of glucose and other sugars by bacteria or yeasts

fossil: the remains of an animal, plant, or other organism preserved in rocks

genes: the basic units of inheritance that control the characteristics of an organism

genetic engineering: the scientific manipulation of genetic material

genetics: the study of inheritance and its units, called genes

germs: microorganisms capable of causing disease

immunity: the ability to resist infection by viruses, bacteria, and other microorganisms that carry disease

immunization: the process of conferring immunity, particularly by inoculation

inoculation: introducing microorganisms into living tissues to produce immunity

microorganisms: single-celled organisms that can only be seen with a microscope

nucleus: the central compartment of a cell that controls the characteristics and growth of the cell

organisms: any living animals or plants

pasteurization: the heating of beverages or foods to destroy harmful microorganisms

reproduction: the process by which an organism produces its offspring

species: a group of living organisms that can interbreed to produce fertile offspring

vaccination: a method of giving immunity against infectious disease caused by bacteria or viruses

viruses: tiny parasitic organisms that reproduce inside the cell of their host

zoology: the scientific study of animal life

Index

LIGHTBOX

SUPPLEMENTARY RESOURCES

Click on the plus icon found in the bottom left corner of each spread to open additional teacher resources.

- Download and print the book's quizzes and activities
- Access curriculum correlations
- Explore additional web applications that enhance the Lightbox experience

LIGHTBOX DIGITAL TITLES
Packed full of integrated media

VIDEOS

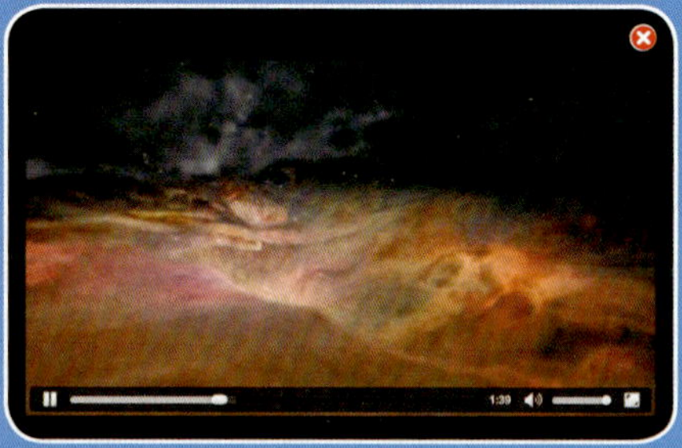

INTERACTIVE MAPS

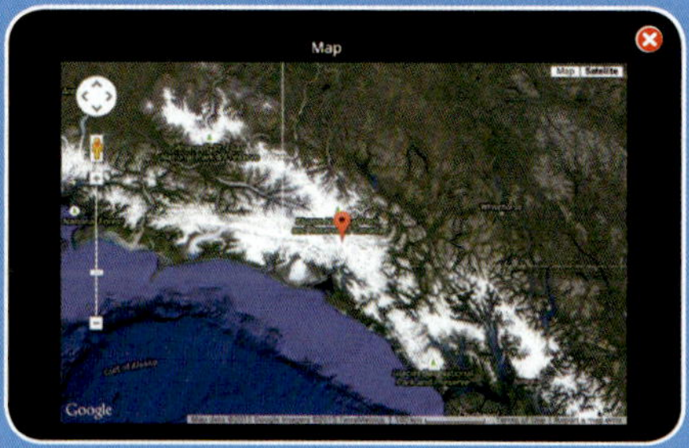

WEBLINKS

SLIDESHOWS

QUIZZES

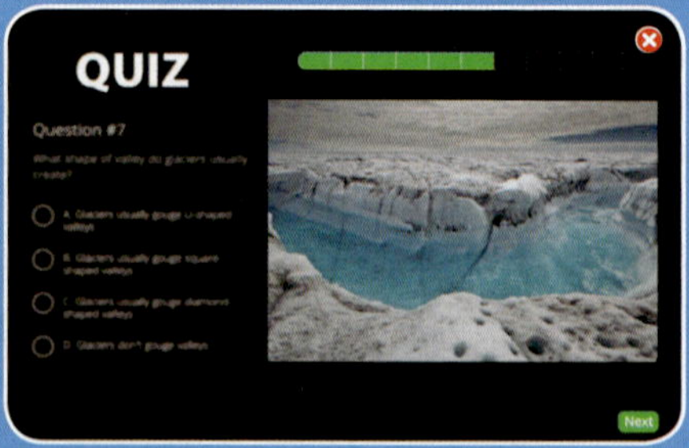

OPTIMIZED FOR
- ✓ TABLETS
- ✓ WHITEBOARDS
- ✓ COMPUTERS
- ✓ AND MUCH MORE!

Published by Smartbook Media Inc.
350 5th Avenue, 59th Floor New York, NY 10118
Website: www.openlightbox.com

Library of Congress Control Number: 2018937314

ISBN 978-1-5105-3757-6 (hardcover)
ISBN 978-1-5105-3758-3 (multi-user eBook)

Printed in Brainerd, Minnesota, United States
1 2 3 4 5 6 7 8 9 0 22 21 20 19 18

062018
121217

Project Coordinator: Jared Siemens
Designer: Ana María Vidal

Every reasonable effort has been made to trace ownership and to obtain permission to reprint copyright material. The publisher would be pleased to have any errors or omissions brought to its attention so that they may be corrected in subsequent printings. The publisher acknowledges Getty Images, Shutterstock, iStock, Dreamstime, and Alamy as its primary image suppliers for this title.